✧ *Companions for the Journey* ✧

Praying with
John of the Cross

✧ *Companions for the Journey* ✧

Praying with John of the Cross

by
Wayne Simsic

Saint Mary's Press
Christian Brothers Publications
Winona, Minnesota

For
✧ *Sr. Mercia Madigan,* ✧
who taught me by example
the wisdom of self-giving and
the power of unconditional love

The publishing team for this book included Carl Koch, FSC, development editor; Amy Schlumpf Manion, manuscript editor and typesetter; Elaine Kohner, illustrator; pre-press, printing, and binding by the graphics division of Saint Mary's Press.

The psalm on page 48 and the excerpt on pages 86–87 are from *Psalms Anew: In Inclusive Language*, compiled by Nancy Schreck and Maureen Leach (Winona, MN: Saint Mary's Press, 1986), pages 51 and 16, respectively. Copyright © 1986 by Saint Mary's Press. All rights reserved.
    The scriptural quotation on page 56 is from the New Revised Standard Version of the Bible. Copyright © 1989 by the Division of Christian Education of the National Council of the Churches of Christ in the United States of America. All rights reserved.
    The scriptural material found on page 77 is freely adapted and is not to be understood or used as an official translation of the Bible.
    All other scriptural quotations used in this book are from the New Jerusalem Bible. Copyright © 1985 by Darton, Longman & Todd, London; and Doubleday, a division of Bantam, Doubleday, Dell Publishing Group, New York. Used with permission.

The acknowledgments continue on page 100.

Printed in the United States of America

Printing: 6 5 4 3 2 1

Year: 1999 98 97 96 95 94 93

ISBN 0-88489-290-5

✧ Contents ✧

✧ Foreword ✧

Companions for the Journey

Just as food is required for human life, so are companions. Indeed, the word *companions* comes from two Latin words: *com,* meaning "with," and *panis,* meaning "bread." Companions nourish our heart, mind, soul, and body. They are also the people with whom we can celebrate the sharing of bread.

Perhaps the most touching stories in the Bible are about companionship: the Last Supper, the wedding feast at Cana, the sharing of the loaves and the fishes, and Jesus' breaking of bread with the disciples on the road to Emmaus. Each incident of companionship with Jesus revealed more about his mercy, love, wisdom, suffering, and hope. When Jesus went to pray in the Garden of Olives, he craved the companionship of the Apostles. They let him down. But God sent the Spirit to inflame the hearts of the Apostles, and they became faithful companions to Jesus and to one another.

Throughout history, other faithful companions have followed Jesus and the Apostles. These saints and mystics have also taken the journey from conversion, through suffering, to resurrection. Just as they were inspired by the holy people who went before them, so too may you take them as your companions as you walk on your spiritual journey.

The Companions for the Journey series is a response to the spiritual hunger of Christians. This series makes available the rich spiritual teachings of mystics and guides whose wisdom can help us on our pilgrimages. As you complete the last meditation in each volume, it is hoped that you will feel supported, challenged, and affirmed by a soul-companion on your spiritual journey.

The spiritual hunger that has emerged over the last twenty years is a great sign of renewal in Christian life. People fill retreat programs and workshops on topics in spirituality. The demand for spiritual directors exceeds the number available. Interest in the lives and writings of saints and mystics is increasing as people search for models of whole and holy Christian life.

Praying with John of the Cross

Praying with John of the Cross is more than just a book about John's spirituality. This book seeks to engage you in praying in the way that John did about issues and themes that were central to his experience. Each meditation can enlighten your understanding of his spirituality and lead you to reflect on your own experience.

The goal of *Praying with John of the Cross* is that you will discover John's rich spirituality and integrate his spirit and wisdom into your relationship with God, with your brothers and sisters, and with your own heart and mind.

Suggestions for Praying with John of the Cross

Meet John, a fascinating companion for your pilgrimage, by reading the introduction to this book, which begins on page 13. It provides a brief biography of John and an outline of the major themes of his spirituality.

Once you meet John, you will be ready to pray with him and to encounter God, your sisters and brothers, and yourself in new and wonderful ways. To help your prayer, here are some suggestions that have been part of the tradition of Christian spirituality:

Create a sacred space. Jesus said, "'When you pray, go to your private room, shut yourself in, and so pray to your [God] who is in that secret place, and your [God] who sees all that is done in secret will reward you'" (Matthew 6:6). Solitary prayer is best done in a place where you can have privacy and silence, both of which can be luxuries in the life of busy people.

If privacy and silence are not possible, create a quiet, safe place within yourself, perhaps while riding to and from work, while sitting in line at the dentist's office, or while waiting for someone. Do the best you can, knowing that a loving God is present everywhere. Whether the meditations in this book are used for solitary prayer or with a group, try to create a prayerful mood with candles, meditative music, an open Bible, or a crucifix.

Open yourself to the power of prayer. Every human experience has a religious dimension. All of life is suffused with God's presence. So remind yourself that God is present as you begin your period of prayer. Do not worry about distractions. If something keeps intruding during your prayer, spend some time talking with God about it. Be flexible because God's Spirit blows where it will.

Prayer can open your mind and widen your vision. Be open to new ways of seeing God, people, and yourself. As you open yourself to the Spirit of God, different emotions are evoked, such as sadness from tender memories, or joy from a celebration recalled. Our emotions are messages from God that can tell us much about our spiritual quest. Also, prayer strengthens our will to act. Through prayer, God can touch our will and empower us to live according to what we know is true.

Finally, many of the meditations in this book will call you to employ your memories, your imagination, and the circumstances of your life as subjects for prayer. The great mystics and saints realized that they had to use all their resources to know God better. Indeed, God speaks to us continually and touches us constantly. We must learn to listen and feel with all the means that God has given us.

Come to prayer with an open mind, heart, and will.

Preview each meditation before beginning. After you have placed yourself in God's presence, spend a few moments previewing the readings and especially the reflection activities. Several reflection activities are given in each meditation because different styles of prayer appeal to different personalities or personal needs. **Note that each meditation has more**

reflection activities than can be done during one prayer period. Therefore, select only one or two reflection activities each time you use a meditation. Do not feel compelled to complete all the reflection activities.

Read meditatively. Each meditation offers you a story about John and a reading from his writings. Take your time reading. If a particular phrase touches you, stay with it. Relish its feelings, meanings, and concerns.

Use the reflections. Following the readings is a short reflection in commentary form, which is meant to give perspective to the readings. Then you are offered several ways of meditating on the readings and the theme of the prayer. You may be familiar with the different methods of meditating, but in case you are not, they are described briefly here:

✦ *Repeated short prayer or mantra:* One means of focusing your prayer is to use a mantra, or "prayer word." The mantra may be a single word or a short phrase taken from the readings or from the Scriptures. For example, a short prayer for meditation 1 in this book is simply the phrase "fire of love." Repeated slowly in harmony with your breathing, the mantra helps you center your heart and mind on one action or attribute of God.

✦ *Lectio divina:* This type of meditation is "divine studying," a concentrated reflection on the word of God or the wisdom of a spiritual writer. Most often in *lectio divina*, you will be invited to read one of the passages several times and then concentrate on one or two sentences, pondering their meaning for you and their effect on you. *Lectio divina* commonly ends with formulation of a resolution.

✦ *Guided meditation:* In this type of meditation, our imagination helps us consider alternative actions and likely consequences. Our imagination helps us experience new ways of seeing God, our neighbors, ourselves, and nature. When Jesus told his followers parables and stories, he engaged their imagination. In this book, you will be invited to follow guided meditations.

One way of doing a guided meditation is to read the scene or story several times, until you know the outline and can recall it when you enter into reflection. Or before your prayer time, you may wish to record the meditation on a tape recorder. If so, remember to allow pauses for reflection between phrases and to speak with a slow, peaceful pace and tone. Then, during prayer, when you have finished the readings and the reflection commentary, you can turn on your recording of the meditation and be led through it. If you find your own voice too distracting, ask a friend to make the tape for you.

✦ *Examen of consciousness:* The reflections often will ask you to examine how God has been speaking to you in your past and present experience—in other words, the reflections will ask you to examine your awareness of God's presence in your life.

✦ *Journal writing:* Writing is a process of discovery. If you write for any length of time, stating honestly what is on your mind and in your heart, you will unearth much about who you are, how you stand with your God, what deep longings reside in your soul, and more. In some reflections, you will be asked to write a dialog with Jesus or someone else. If you have never used writing as a means of meditation, try it. Reserve a special notebook for your journal writing. If desired, you can go back to your entries at a future time for an examen of consciousness.

✦ *Action:* Occasionally, a reflection will suggest singing a favorite hymn, going out for a walk, or undertaking some other physical activity. Actions can be meaningful forms of prayer.

Using the Meditations for Group Prayer

If you wish to use the meditations for community prayer, these suggestions may help:

✦ Read the theme to the group. Call the community into the presence of God, using the short opening prayer. Invite one or two participants to read one or both readings. If you use both readings, observe the pause between them.

✦ The reflection commentary may be used as a reading, or it can be deleted, depending on the needs and interests of the group.

✦ Select one of the reflection activities for your group. Allow sufficient time for your group to reflect, to recite a centering prayer or mantra, to accomplish a studying prayer (*lectio divina*), or to finish an examen of consciousness. Depending on the group and the amount of available time, you may want to invite the participants to share their reflections, responses, or petitions with the group.

✦ Reading the passage from the Scriptures may serve as a summary of the meditation.

✦ If a formulated prayer or a psalm is given as a closing, it may be recited by the entire group. Or you may ask participants to offer their own prayers for the closing.

Now you are ready to begin praying with John of the Cross, a faithful and caring companion on this stage of your spiritual journey. It is hoped that you will find him to be a true soul-companion.

CARL KOCH, FSC
Editor

✧ Introduction ✧

John of the Cross: Spiritual Guide

John of the Cross was a poet, mystic, theologian, spiritual director, administrator, and collaborator with Teresa of Ávila in the reform of the Carmelites. Declared a saint in 1726, two hundred years later, Pope Pius XI proclaimed John a Doctor of the Church.

John's message begins with love and longing for God. In "The Spiritual Canticle," John calls out to God:

Where have you hidden,
Beloved, and left me moaning?
> (John of the Cross, "The Spiritual Canticle")

Through his life and writings, John of the Cross repeatedly declared that God's love is meant for and is accessible to all people, and that our life is an ongoing love story—the story of God inviting us to a deeper transforming relationship. "Love," he says, "is the soul's inclination, strength, and power in making its way to God, for love unites it with God" (John of the Cross, "The Living Flame of Love"). Only by responding to this call of love do we begin to let go of the things that keep us from loving more fully.

The transforming love of God involves a person entirely, but we must be free to hear and respond to the mystery at work in our life. John certainly emphasized detachment from all obstacles that hinder a healthy relationship with God, but he always began with the presumption that God is our beloved. Therefore, John speaks to any person who hungers for a spiritual adventure and for a guide who can gently point the way.

Childhood and Youth

John of the Cross was born Juan de Yepes y Alvarez in 1542 in
Fontiveros, Spain, on the feast day of Saint John the Baptist.
Even though this was during what was considered Spain's
Golden Age, the people in the small Castilian farming village
saw mostly poverty, sickness, famine, and early death.

John's father, Gonzalo de Yepes, came from a family of
rich silk merchants but fell into disfavor when, for love alone,
he married Catalina Alvarez, a poor weaver beneath his social
class. Shortly after their marriage, Spain reeled under calami-
ties: a plague of locusts ravaged the countryside and the Spanish government went bankrupt, leaving starving farmers and
village people to fend for themselves. John and his two older
brothers, Francisco and Luis, were born into poverty. When
John was still a child, Gonzalo de Yepes died from a lingering
illness. A year later, Luis died from malnutrition. As "acute
poverty began to press on mother and children like a halter,"
Catalina took her teenage son, Francisco, and the infant, John,
to the province of Toledo, hoping to solicit aid from her hus-
band's family (Crisógono de Jesús, *The Life of St. John of the
Cross*, trans. Kathleen Pond, p. 3). Cruelly, one of Gonzalo's
brothers dismissed her outright, and the other returned Francisco to his mother shortly after agreeing to take him in.

The stricken family moved on to Medina del Campo, a
bustling city northwest of Madrid, where Catalina and her
sons attempted to earn a living as weavers. By the age of nine,
the experience of suffering had taken root in John's life. He
had lost a father and a brother, and, with his remaining family, lived a hand-to-mouth existence. Nevertheless, Catalina
was an extraordinary woman who not only took loving care
of her own children, but helped other needy people, such as
an orphan she found in the streets one day. Francisco, a simple
man, became a compassionate adult who aided poor and sick
people the way his mother did. Some contemporaries considered him to be more holy than John.

John learned to read and write in a kind of vocational
school for orphans and poor children where he received both
food and shelter. He also learned the rudiments of carpentry,
tailoring, wood carving, and painting. For the rest of his life,

John used the practical education he received, and incorporated images from these trades in his writings.

At the school, an important incident occurred that affected John profoundly. One day, while playing with schoolmates in the courtyard of a hospital, he fell into a deep well. His friends feared that he had drowned. John, "however, floated up to the top of the water and asked them to throw him a rope. He tied it round him beneath the arms himself and came out unharmed. . . . Juan Gómez, who lived near the hospital . . . was passing by just when they had brought John out of the well and heard a group of onlookers recounting what had just happened as a miracle wrought by the Blessed Virgin" (Crisógono, *Life*, p. 13). John maintained that, indeed, the Blessed Mother had kept him afloat. After this incident, John sought Mary's help to guide him for the rest of his life.

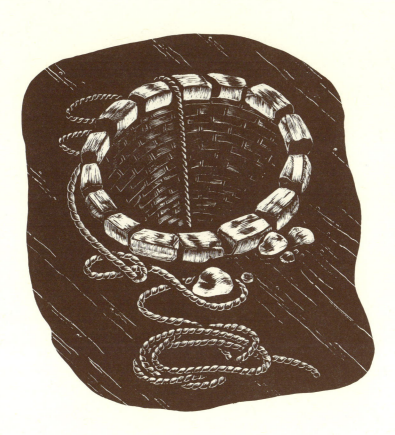

Choosing a Vocation

Early in his adolescence, John left the orphanage school and went to live in the Hospital of the Conception, a hospital specially devoted to victims of the plague and venereal diseases. An understanding administrator who saw John's compassion for sick people guided him. John gently changed bandages, encouraged his patients, and even begged for money in the streets for the hospital.

In exchange for his work as a nurse, John attended a local Jesuit college. For four years he immersed himself in the humanities, studying Latin, Greek, rhetoric, the Spanish classics, and religion. Intellectually gifted, dedicated, and curious, John stayed up late into the night studying.

The administrator of the hospital wanted John to be ordained and to serve as hospital chaplain. Instead, John decided to pursue his growing love for solitude. As a result, he entered the Carmelite order originated by a group of hermits dedicated to Mary and to contemplative life. John took the religious name, Fray Juan de Santo Matía.

The Carmelites sent John to study at the University of Salamanca, one of the finest European universities of the period. He encountered a stimulating intellectual environment and several outstanding teachers. John soon distinguished himself with his knowledge of the Scriptures, patristics (the study of the writings of the church fathers), and systematic theology. Due to his academic accomplishments, his superiors appointed John prefect of studies at the Carmelite College of San Andrés.

However, John's main interests tended toward the spiritual development of the human person, not academic theology. John enthusiastically followed a spiritual discipline that involved fasting, prayer, and various forms of penance. Penitential practices played a large role in spirituality during his era, but John would later urge devout people to forgo excessive penance and concentrate on a more balanced spirituality.

Teresa of Ávila and the Reform of Carmelite Religious Life

Near the end of his university studies, John considered entering a Carthusian monastery where he could have even more solitude. However, he stayed with the Carmelites, who ordained him. Soon John returned to Medina del Campo to say his first Mass, and here he met Teresa of Ávila. Attempting to lead her sisters back to the original rule of the order—regular community life, fasting, silence, poverty, and prayer—Teresa founded renewed monasteries of Carmelite nuns. These communities were referred to as "reform" or "discalced." *Discalced* means "without shoes" or "barefoot," a characteristic common to some religious communities of the time.

> As a result of her personal mystical experience, Teresa envisioned her communities as small groups of friends of Christ and the contemplative life, the way of recollection, as a life of intimacy with Jesus, who continued forever to be human as well as divine. The manner of reciting the Divine Office was now simpler, an hour in the morning and an hour in the evening was set aside for mental prayer, and the nuns lived their day mostly in silence and solitude, engaging, alone in their cells, in the manual labor of spinning to help support themselves. (Kieran Kavanaugh, ed., *John of the Cross: Selected Writings*, p. 14)

To balance their daily living, Teresa incorporated periods of recreation into the rule. During these times, the nuns talked, performed short morality plays, or even danced with castanets.

When Teresa and John encountered one another, Teresa was looking for someone to lead a similar reform among Carmelite friars and had heard about John's spirituality. Soon John shared Teresa's enthusiasm for the formation of observant communities of Carmelite men. Though Teresa was twenty-seven years older than John, they shared wisdom and affection. Speaking of John to her nuns, Teresa once said, "'I am bringing you, ladies, a saint for confessor'" (Crisógono, *Life*, p. 71). They became fast friends.

While John considered Teresa to be his mentor, she recognized him as her spiritual equal. With her great sense of humor, Teresa could also enjoy the earnest John. When the diminuitive John (he stood only four feet eleven inches) and Fray Antonio, an older Carmelite, committed themselves to setting up the newly reformed house, Teresa delightedly quipped, "'Now I have a friar and a half to begin the Reform with!'" (E. Allison Peers, *Spirit of Flame: A Study of St. John of the Cross*, p. 14). Such was their friendship that John kept a portrait of Teresa with him and exchanged poetry with her by letter. They sorely missed each other when separated for too long.

After a brief period of instruction from Teresa, John and two other friars began a reformed community in a small, ramshackle house at Duruelo, not far from Ávila. John also changed his name to Juan de la Cruz, or John of the Cross. His mother, brother, and sister-in-law joined him in Duruelo. John thrived even though the conditions were primitive, and he found the hard manual labor, his apostolate in a neighboring village, and the peaceful rural surroundings perfect for his prayer life.

Soon men wanted to join the reformed community. The little house became too small, but a donor offered money for a new house. John and the brothers helped build a monastery in Mancera, and the Carmelite friars rapidly extended their ministry even further. John served as novice master to the new recruits. In 1570, John moved to Pastrana, where another reformed house had opened. Growth continued, and the superior put John in charge of a house of studies at the fledgling university in Alcalá de Henares.

A year later, at Teresa's request, John was assigned to be confessor and spiritual director to the Convent of the Incarnation in Ávila, where the ecclesiastical superior had appointed Teresa as prioress. Her wisdom, zeal, and firm hand were needed to renew a community badly divided and demoralized. She knew that she would need the help of a kindred spirit like John. For the next five years, John lived in a hut at the edge of the property. He said Mass, heard confessions, taught catechism to local children, and gave spiritual direction to both nuns and laypeople. He learned a great deal about God's subtle way of influencing souls and helped Teresa herself to enter deeper into her prayer life. Teresa declared that he was an incomparable spiritual director.

John's Imprisonment

The reform that was originally supported by some leaders in the Carmelite Order became a source of disagreement and anger. John stayed out of the wrangling, but still became the focus of attention due to his role as founding member of the first reformed house. The jealously and tension that surrounded his position as chaplain and confessor to the nuns, and close collaborator with Teresa also contributed.

A meeting of the Carmelites condemned the reform movement. The unsuspecting John was arrested on 2 December 1577 and led off to Toledo. There, the unreformed Carmelites declared him to be a rebel, and threw him into a small cell in their monastery:

> Here Fray John was brought on a winter's day. . . . All he had with him was his breviary. Soon he would feel the effects of the terrible cold of Toledo . . . and would find the skin coming off his toes from frost-bite. Here he was to spend nine months, solitary, hungry, in an atmosphere with an unpleasant smell, wasting away . . . with no other light than that which came in through the diminutive opening high up in the wall of the tiny cell. (Crisógono, *Life*, p. 103)

He was flogged, starved, and told to forsake his commitment to the primitive rule. These nine months of suffering became John's dark night of the soul.

In the midst of his stark emptiness, images flowed from the depths of his soul, which later poured out in his poetic masterpieces, "The Dark Night of the Soul" and "The Spiritual Canticle."

> Where have you hidden,
> Beloved, and left me moaning?
> You fled like the stag

After wounding me;
I went out calling you, and you were gone.

Shepherds, you that go
Up through the sheepfolds to the hill,
If by chance you see
Him I love most,
Tell him that I sicken, suffer, and die.

(John of the Cross, "The Spiritual Canticle")

Meanwhile, Teresa wrote the Spanish king, "'I am terribly distressed to see our friars in such hands. . . . As for this friar [John of the Cross], who is such a true servant of God, he is so weak, after all that he has suffered, that I fear for his life" (Peers, *Spirit of Flame*, p. 41).

One night, through his own watchfulness, perhaps with the connivance of a sympathetic friar left to guard him, some planning, and unusual circumstances, John escaped and hid with the Discalced nuns in Toledo. Even though John's enemies kept guard on the monastery, the nuns saw that John received the medical help he needed and spirited him away from his captors.

Leadership and Writing

Meanwhile, after a long and complicated process, the Discalced became an independent community (though not a separate order), and were allowed to govern themselves. The Discalced friars named John superior of their monastery at El Calvario in the region of Andalusia. Its isolation would provide John some protection from his enemies. John gladly retreated to this place of great natural beauty. His love for creation's majesty deepened throughout his life, and at El Calvario he could often be found completely absorbed while gazing at a landscape. He urged the friars to relax in the woods and countryside, and he himself found a place to pray on the side of a mountain where the view was spectacular. Priors from other monasteries would visit John unexpectedly and find him working outdoors in the garden, his hands caked with dirt. Still, John never ceased to minister to people by teaching, catechizing, and giving spiritual direction.

After a year at El Calvario, John assumed direction of the order's college at Baeza. From there he moved to Granada and became prior of a monastery overlooking the Sierra Nevada and situated next to the magnificent Alhambra Palace of the Moors. Never averse to hard work, he designed the monastery and undertook the construction of an aqueduct to water the gardens so food could be grown for the friars and poor people. He also built the cloister. Both he and his brother, Francisco, made the bricks and laid them. The people of Granada loved the prior and, knowing his shyness, brought in a painter to observe him secretly and paint his portrait.

His six years in Granada were perhaps the richest time in John's life. Besides his duties as prior, he was a spiritual director for a community of reformed Carmelite nuns. Their questions about the spiritual life inspired his writing. He completed "The Spiritual Canticle," wrote "The Living Flame of Love," and finished commentaries on "The Ascent of Mount Carmel" and "The Dark Night of the Soul."

In time, he was elected vicar provincial, traveled frequently, founded seven monasteries, and gave spiritual direction and conferences. While visiting communities, he pitched in with manual work—building stone walls, making bricks, or tending the vegetables. He also wrote brief plays that the communities could perform for feast days. And, like his mentor and friend, Teresa, John would spring into dance or lift his voice in song when his love for God overtook him.

The Later Years

In 1588, John became prior in Segovia and was elected a councillor to the vicar general, Nicolás Doria. When he differed with the domineering vicar general, John fell out of favor and was sent to an isolated monastery as punishment. For his part, John enjoyed the solitude and the opportunity to pray. However, while John prayed and ministered quietly, two friars began building a case against him in an attempt to have him dismissed from the Discalced community. The process halted when a fever and serious inflammation of the leg attacked John.

The prior of the monastery where he lay sick treated John shabbily. Surgery on his leg proved fruitless. Realizing that he was about to die, John asked the prior to forgive him since he had not intended to cause trouble or inconvenience. Such gentle compassion melted the prior's resentment and, in tears, he confessed sorrow for the ill treatment of his guest. Shortly after midnight and the ringing of the bell for matins, John asked, "'What are they ringing for?' . . . When they told him that it was for matins, . . . he exclaimed joyfully, 'Glory be to God for I shall say them in heaven.' He put his lips to the crucifix he was holding in his hands, and said slowly, '*In manus tuas, Domine, commendo spiritum meum*' [Into your hands, O Lord, I commend my spirit], and breathed his last." (Crisógono, *Life*, pp. 303–304).

John, the Poet

John wrote three major poems: "The Dark Night of the Soul," "The Spiritual Canticle," and "The Living Flame of Love." The images in these poems are the seeds that germinated into his prose writings. To explore images such as "living flame of love," "secret ladder," "absent lover," "dark night," "wounded heart," and "silent music" within our own experience is to discover the energy of John's teaching. Poetry was not simply an art form for John. Rather he wrote poetry to express his deepest awareness of God's love.

Meditating on John's poetry is essential to understanding and appreciating his spirituality. John wrote extensive commentaries on his poems, but John himself would probably advise reading the poems first because they reflect not only his personality but the immediacy and power of his love relationship with God. As with any great poetry, John's poems need to be read receptively, letting the images penetrate the imagination and resonate with one's experience. The images that John uses in his poems come from the depths of the unconscious where they are linked to the common ground of all human experience. As a result, everyone can identify with them if they remain open on intuitive and emotional levels. John of the Cross urges us, "Read [the poems] with the simplicity of the spirit of knowledge and love they contain" (John of the Cross, "The Spiritual Canticle"). John's poetry reveals the story of his spiritual journey in a way that allows us to discover the story of our own journey to God.

The poems read like a personal autobiography. Most are written in the first person singular. John was aware that his experience was indefinable. In fact this is a recurrent theme of his: "Who can describe the understanding He gives to loving souls in whom He dwells?" (John of the Cross, "The Spiritual Canticle"). Yet, he felt the overwhelming need to express his experience of the Spirit, to embody it, and to charge it with emotion in his poetry.

Central Themes in John's Spirituality

On fire with love: John's spirituality centers on his passion for God. The fire of his love for the Divine burns throughout his writings. John formed his life so that it answered the Gospel injunction to seek the Reign of God, and to love God with one's whole soul, heart, mind, and strength. John's asceticism should be understood as a willing response to the overwhelming presence of Divine love in his life.

Compassion for poor and sick people: John cared for hospital patients in his youth and showed deep compassion for anyone in need. His periods spent in solitude intensified his empathy and dedication to service. During a year of famine, John ordered that none of the poor people who came to the doors of the monastery should be sent away with empty hands.

Sensitivity to spiritual needs: John's apostolate focused on his zeal for spiritual direction. He felt that people were best served through gentle direction that drew them to love God. He companioned anyone who came to him, including simple and unlearned folk. He directed both religious and lay people, heard confessions of villagers, and taught catechism to youth.

Detachment: John saw that being free from inordinate desires was necessary in order to love God. Selfish hearts lose their way and wander aimlessly, unable to find their true home in God. John taught that we should love everything God has made, in a way that reflects not our interest but God's interest. As a result the heart must be progressively purified of all excessive attachments through the fire of Divine love. This purification and letting go leads to the dark night of the senses and, eventually, the dark night of the soul.

Humility: John sought no position of distinction in the order and preferred to stay in the background when others became embroiled in political concerns. He did the most menial tasks, such as sweeping floors or laying brick. When someone asked him why a person in his position spent so much time in the garden he answered, "'I am not so important as that . . . for I am the son of a poor weaver'" (Crisógono, *Life*, p. 211). In short, John knew and accepted who he was before God.

Trust in God: John once advised a woman who was experiencing God's absence to trust in God and the signs that God offers, and to be at peace for all would be well. Subsequently, John had to take his own advice. When John was imprisoned, he accepted the unwarranted suffering that almost took his life and offered himself to God each day.

His insistence on relying on God often clashed with common sense. On one occasion, a friar told John that they had no money for food and sought permission to search for supplies. John refused permission three times and told the friar that God would provide. Soon after, a woman came to the door of the monastery bearing gifts to the community.

Love of solitude: Solitude nourished John's spiritual strength and his intimacy with God. He would steal off to caves, forests, unused rooms—any place he could find silence and privacy to embrace God without reserve. In solitude, the wounds of love drew him toward complete absorption in

God. However, his desire for solitude did not clash with his apostolic duties. Each enlightened, inspired, and gave strength to the other.

Devotion to Mary: From his boyhood, John received signs that Mary guided him. Rescued from the deep well, he had a vision of the Mother of God. That image of Mary lit a secret flame in his heart and directed his key decisions. At the end of his life, he believed that Mary was taking his hand and leading him into eternal life.

Praying with John

John saw meditation as the first step toward union with God. Meditative prayer relies on the use of reason, memory, imagination, and will. It focuses our energies and directs them gradually toward God. Authentic meditation strengthens one's reliance on God alone.

A higher stage of prayer occurs when God's transforming love places one in a state of contemplation: "The more degrees of love it has, the more deeply it enters into God and centers itself in Him" (John of the Cross, "The Living Flame of Love"). Unlike meditation, a person feels no inclination to understand or imagine God, but instead only rests in the loving awareness of God. To rest is to allow one's entire being to be absorbed by love. So this form of prayer may be simply longing for God.

Through meditation we can see how to live charitably and justly, although we usually realize that we cannot reform our lives with only our efforts. The practice of meditation, then, may draw a person into contemplation. Contemplation often seems like a dark night in which God completes the process of purifying us from all that hinders the deepest love. John cautions us to ground our lives in the virtues through meditation and action as a fitting response to the call of grace. God will call us to contemplation when we are ready.

John for Today

Today, people of all ages and from all walks of life hunger for a God they can experience as transforming love. John speaks to anyone who is authentically intent on searching for God and is willing to prove love for God through sacrifice. John's gift is the ability to guide us through spiritual life without taking detours that could cause harm to our soul.

As a guide, God respects us, trusts us, and gives us the freedom to make our own choices. God does not force an opinion, but hopes that we approach spirituality in the way that best suits our needs. After all, God's way is hidden. "Who can describe the understanding He gives to loving souls in whom He dwells," John wrote to Madre Ana de Jesús, prioress at Granada (John of the Cross, "The Spiritual Canticle").

Though our own experience of God's love may be different from John's, each of us can benefit from John's spirituality because God loves each of us. That is why John's words ring true for us and resonate in our hearts long after we have heard them.

✧ Meditation 1 ✧

Living Flame of Love

Theme: The heart of John's spirituality recognizes that God's love invites us to an intimate, passionate, transforming union with the Beloved.

Opening prayer: All-loving God, teach me to remain open to the deep stirrings of love that rise throughout the day and call me into your presence. I pray with John:

O living flame of love
That tenderly wounds my soul
In its deepest center! Since
Now you are not oppressive,
Now Consummate! if it be your will:
Tear through the veil of this sweet encounter!

. . . .

O lamps of fire!
In whose splendors
The deep caverns of feeling,
Once obscure and blind,
Now give forth, so rarely, so exquisitely,
Both warmth and light to their beloved.
          (John of the Cross, "The Living Flame of Love")

About John

John wanted all people to believe that God loves passionately and without reserve. John knew that even the simplest gift in creation was a sign of God's unfailing love for all and an invitation to love in return. The Carmelite nuns that John directed were well aware of his own absorption by the love of God.

> Merely by looking at him they observed that "he had his heart absorbed in God." It seemed as if he left behind him all his cares as prior and member of the General Council. He never knew what he had had to eat. The nuns would ask him this intentionally, and he, making a great effort to remember, would say "Wait, now, wait . . ."—and he had to give up the attempt. At times, as if he were constantly being drawn towards interior things, he lost the thread of what he was saying and said . . . "Tell me what we were speaking of." On the other hand, when in their conversations which were usually about God, temporal affairs, settled in a few words, intervened, he cut the matter short quickly, saying to the prioress, "Let us leave these trifles and speak of God." (Crisógono, *Life*, p. 265)

Pause: Recall a time when you felt the fire of God's love suddenly fill your life in the middle of the ordinary events of the day.

John's Words

For John, spirituality is an ongoing love affair with the God of truth and love:

> Love is the soul's inclination, strength, and power in making its way to God, for love unites it with God. The more degrees of love it has, the more deeply it enters into God and centers itself in Him. (John of the Cross, "The Living Flame of Love")

> Hence we can compare the soul in its ordinary condition in this state of transformation of love to the log of wood

that is ever immersed in fire, and the acts of this soul to the flame that blazes up from the fire of love. The more intense the fire of union, the more vehemently does this fire burst into flames. The acts of the will are united to this flame and ascend, carried away and absorbed in the flame of the Holy Spirit. (John of the Cross, "The Living Flame of Love")

Reflection

The constant presence of love, the Holy Spirit, within the ordinary events of life—a beautiful landscape, an act of kindness, a talk with a friend, or silent prayer—could set John's soul on fire. He opened his heart completely to love's influence. John's relationships with his mother, brother, the friars and nuns, and Teresa of Ávila nourished his love of God. The Holy Spirit, the source of all love, spread through John back to them.

In talking about love with the nuns, John mapped out a path to union with God where selfishness decreases and love for God increases. At the end of this path, a person becomes love itself, and at death is united with the God of love. John realized that before we can be fully alight in the purification and transformation of our lives by "the living flame of love," we must become sensitive to the call of love. Without the strength and hope fueled by love, the fire of spiritual growth would die. John tells us that the heat of God's love smolders at the core of the heart, waiting to flame. Similarly, Paul tells the Hebrews, "our God is a consuming fire" (12:29).

✧ Light some candles, or start a fire in your fireplace. Relax, breathe deeply and rhythmically, repeating the phrase *fire of love* with each breath you inhale. Allow the words to draw you toward the warmth of God's love at the center of your being.

✧ List the pure, undeserved gifts of love that the Holy Spirit has offered you in your life: people, talents, possessions, and so on. Once you have drawn up the list, repeat it to yourself slowly, thinking of the value of each gift, and offering each one back to God.

✧ Invitations to be aflame with God's love come throughout the day—in a conversation with a friend, in the brilliance of a sunrise, in the expression on a child's face. Take time to recall and reflect on the small invitations of love you have experienced the last few days.

✧ Imagine that your life story begins, "Once upon a time . . ." You are searching for the grail of perfect love, and this story tells of your quest. Using the scenarios and questions below, let the story of your life unfold:

✦ Imagine that you awaken one night and realize that you feel a strong urge to begin a quest for a treasure of great value. Have you ever felt conscious of deep, evocative goals and values in your life, of longing for profound happiness? Describe the times this awareness occurred and what effect it had on you.

✦ See yourself traveling through a dark forest. You lose your way. Have you ever strayed from the path of love, and grown fearful that the Holy Spirit was absent in your life?

✦ Your path unexpectedly crosses the paths of others. Who are the individuals who have awakened you to deeper levels of love? Describe how these people gave you help and courage on your quest.

✦ Along the way you suddenly find a powerful symbol that accesses powerful inner resources when you need them. What things in your life are sources of strength for you in difficult times?

✦ Finally, you discover the treasure that has eluded you, but in the process, your life has been transformed. What is your vision of the ultimate love that, on occasion, dispels the darkness of your life—a love in which you hope to find complete happiness?

✧ We are often lonely for God and do not recognize our loneliness. Listen to a favorite piece of music, and once the music has calmed your mind, allow yourself to feel the deep ache you may have for God. Let your feelings take the form of a prayer if this seems appropriate.

God's Word

And now a lawyer stood up and, to test [Jesus], asked, "Master, what must I do to inherit eternal life?" He said to him, "What is written in the Law? What is your reading of it?" He replied, "You must love the Lord your God with all your heart, with all your soul, with all your strength, and with all your mind, and your neighbour as yourself." Jesus said to him, "You have answered right, do this and life is yours." (Luke 10:25–28)

Closing prayer: Conclude your meditation with these lines from John's poem, "The Living Flame of Love."

How gently and lovingly
You wake in my heart,
Where in secret you dwell alone;
And by your sweet breathing,
Filled with good and glory,
How tenderly you swell my heart with love.
(John of the Cross, "The Living Flame of Love")

✧ Meditation 2 ✧

Trusting in God

Theme: As the fire of love grew in John's heart, he began to trust God's love more surely. This trust progressively freed him from anxiety and fear, and gave him courage.

Opening prayer: Ever-present Mystery, I welcome you into my life. Set my soul on fire with love, so that I may trust you more and more.

About John

John was known for his willingness to focus on God in his thoughts and conversation, trusting that other things, like food, would be provided in their own time. The following story is an example of this.

> The procurator of the monastery came to tell Fray John that there was nothing with which to buy food to make a meal for the friars. As usual, [John] told him that God would provide. After a short time the procurator returned, urging that he should authorize him to go out in search of provisions, but Fray John again refused him permission. . . . The procurator came back for a third time, but Fray John persisted in his refusal. When the procurator had gone away [John] told his penitent [a young woman, Juana, who had come to him for confession] that

he had refused the permission three times because people were already coming with money as alms for the friars. This was a fact—as she went out of the church Juana met a woman who was bringing four ducats in alms for the monastery. (Crisógono, *Life*, p. 207)

Pause: Recall a time when you put your own cares into God's hands.

John's Words

In the following letter, John offers consolation to a woman who was experiencing spiritual darkness and emptiness, and who felt that God had abandoned her.

> While you are in darkness and emptiness of spiritual poverty, you think that everyone and everything are failing you. This is not surprising, for then it also seems to you that God is failing you too. But nothing is wanting to you, nor have you any need to consult me about anything, nor have you reason to do so; for all is merely suspicion without a cause. He who does not want any other thing than God does not walk in darkness, however dark and poor he finds himself. . . . You are in a good way. Be quiet and rejoice. Who are you to be anxious over yourself? You would do well to stop. . . .
>
> . . . Be glad and trust God, who has given you signs that you can very well do so [survive in the darkness] and ought to do so; and if you do not, it will not be surprising that [God] should be vexed, seeing you behave so foolishly, when [God] is taking you where it is best for you and has put you in so safe a place. Do not seek for any way but this and calm your soul, for all is well. (Crisógono, *Life*, pp. 207–208)

Reflection

Restlessness, anxiety, and fear dim our focus on God's will and sap our strength to carry it out. John encouraged people not to worry or be afraid because God accepts their problems and would provide what was best for them in the final analysis. John quietly consoles us with this fact and assures us that peace will come.

John advised those who came to him for counsel that they would enjoy peace of heart much more if they would trust completely in divine Providence. He established the monastery in Duruelo in a run-down farmhouse with only some documents and a few necessities. He worked hard planning and building the aqueduct at Granada, but knew that God sent the water. All along he knew that he was in God's hands. Ultimately, we are always in God's hands.

✧ Slowly reread the advice that John gave to the woman who felt spiritually empty. Bring to mind some situation that right now bothers you and over which you wish you had more control. Let all aspects of the situation register. Then read John's advice again in light of your own troubles. Meditate on his advice to you.

✧ List some of your worries and fears. Then ask yourself how each worry or fear controls you, affects your mood, keeps you from focusing on things that you want to accomplish, and drains you of joy and peace.

Discuss each worry and fear with God and then offer each one back to God. Ask God to take care of your apprehensions.

✧ Part of God's providence is the family, friends, generous strangers, talents, and skills God gives to us. List all of these gifts that God has provided to you, and then praise God for them.

✧ At some point in your life you may have felt abandoned by God—at the death of a parent or close friend, with the loss of a job, upon recognition of your limitations or some vulnerability. John constantly challenges us to relinquish control and trust in someone greater.

✦ Did you turn to God in trust after encountering a major impasse in your life?

✦ Would you have been better off letting go and trusting God more?
✦ Recall one of the times that you gave up and realized that your own efforts caused frustration.
✦ Describe this event in writing, recalling the feelings and insights that came with it.

God's Word

So do not worry; do not say, "What are we to eat? What are we to drink? What are we to wear?" It is the gentiles who set their hearts on all these things. [God] knows you need them all. Set your hearts on [the Reign of God] first, and on God's saving justice, and all these other things will be given you as well. So do not worry about tomorrow: tomorrow will take care of itself. Each day has enough trouble of its own. (Matthew 6:31–34)

Closing prayer: God, give me the courage to face my anxieties and fears, and to hand them over to you throughout the day.

Compassion

Theme: John learned early in his life to be compassionate to people in need. As love burned brighter within him, the warmth of his compassion grew likewise.

Opening prayer: Loving God, may I act with compassion toward my sisters and brothers just as you have been compassionate to me.

About John

As a boy, John learned compassion from his mother as she cared for people even more needy than she was. As a young man, John nursed in a hospital for poor people afflicted with the plague and venereal diseases. The physical and psychological suffering that he witnessed in the hospital heightened his sensitivity to others.

> Though some of them were in terrible condition, he did all he could for them. Their open wounds and the anger and rejection they often expressed did not keep him from fulfilling his function. He would hold the weaker ones up to feed or bathe them and change their bandages when necessary. Touching them would certainly have repelled many others but [John] was determined not to flinch. He wanted them to see that he was there to help them and he

showed it by coming close to them. (Richard P. Hardy, *Search for Nothing: The Life of John of the Cross*, p. 14)

John not only sympathized with poor people, but he acted to help them. He was not embarrassed to beg alms to provide for needy people when necessary.

One day he came into the convent to exercise his ministry and saw that a nun who was sweeping the cloister was bare-footed. She was not going without shoes for a penance, it was because she had none. Fray John left the convent, went up to the city and asked some charitable persons for money which he afterwards handed to the nun to buy a pair of shoes. (Crisógono, *Life*, pp. 75–76)

Pause: List opportunities that you have to help people who are in need.

John's Words

A priest, who knew the saint intimately, wrote the following recollection of John's comments.

[John] said that it is an evident truth that compassion for one's neighbour increases in proportion as the soul is united to God by love. For the more the soul loves, the more does it desire that this same God should be loved and honoured by all [people]; and the more this desire increases, the more does it work to that end, both in prayer and in all other necessary exercises which it can undertake. (Bruno, *St. John of the Cross*, ed. Benedict Zimmerman, p. 290)

Reflection

All compassionate love comes from God's grace. As we love our sisters and brothers, our love for God blossoms. As we learn to love God, we reach out to other people in love. When we fail to love God, we hold back our love for others.

John urged his listeners to be channels of God's love, always ready to reach out in response to the gifts they had received. The world becomes less dark and forbidding the more we offer the light of our heart and the help of our hands.

✧ Reread the section "About John." How do John's actions make you feel? What response can you incorporate into your life?

✧ Compassion for other people seeks expression. List a few of the times that you have opened your heart, hands, ears, eyes, and voice in response to the needs of other people. Thank God in prayer for the gift of these opportunities to act compassionately.

✧ Who is the one person in your life that could use more care and attention from you? How are you being asked to reach out to this person? Have you hesitated? If so, why? Ask God for the grace to overcome any resistance in your heart so that you can act in charity.

✧ If you have had the opportunity to care for an ailing family member or been involved in any service programs, reflect on these questions: How did these experiences change me? Did the warmth of my compassion increase?

✧ Recall all those who are in need: family, friends, enemies, acquaintances, or strangers. In each case, ponder the action you could take to assist each one in his or her need. Then offer prayers on each one's behalf. Take action if you can.

God's Word

Be compassionate just as your [God] is compassionate. Do not judge, and you will not be judged; do not condemn, and you will not be condemned; forgive, and you will be forgiven. Give, and there will be gifts for you: a full measure, pressed down, shaken together, and overflowing, will be poured into your lap; because the standard you use will be the standard used for you. (Luke 6:36–38)

Closing prayer: God, give me the insight and patience to see the needs of other people, and the fire of love to respond with compassion.

✧ Meditation 4 ✧

Enjoying Nature

Theme: A deep love for nature opens our heart to God. As we grow in love for God, we cherish more fully God's manifestation in nature.

Opening prayer: Creator God, cleanse my eyes so that I can see your presence in the beauty and mystery of the natural world.

About John

John could be found in the middle of the woods praying with his arms outstretched, or looking out the window of his room, transfixed by a wide sky dancing with light and casting a spell over the countryside. He was often so immersed in nature that he remained in a trance for long periods of time. His friars respected this form of prayer and would leave him alone with nature and God.

When John was at a monastery outside Segovia, he found a special place for solitude:

Half-way up the rock there was a small, natural cave, low and narrow, which opened out of the living rock. It was surrounded by broom, lavender and brambles. Here [John] liked to come to make his prayer. The views were magnificent and there was an atmosphere of quiet and silence. The air was shot with light, the horizons stretched to infinity. Fray John never tired of being here. . . . When he came down they noticed that he was so absorbed in divine things that he could scarcely attend to what was said to him. At other times, instead of going up to the rock, he went to a small hermitage hidden in the wood. (Crisógono, *Life*, pp. 254–255)

Pause: Using your memory and imagination, return to a favorite place in nature and rest there for a time.

John's Words

Natural images sifted through John's imagination and embedded themselves in the deeper levels of his mind. When he looked for ways to express his love for God, they poured out of his heart.

> Seeking my love
> I will head for the mountains and for watersides,
> I will not gather flowers,
> Nor fear wild beasts;
> I will go beyond strong men and frontiers.
>
> O woods and thickets
> Planted by the hand of my beloved!
> O green meadow,
> Coated, bright with flowers.
> Tell me, has he passed by you?
>
> Pouring out a thousand graces,
> He passed these groves in haste;
> And having looked at them,
> With his image alone,
> Clothed them in beauty.
> (John of the Cross, "The Spiritual Canticle")

Reflection

John passionately embraced the natural world. The grand sweep of a landscape could overwhelm him, and he could be found gazing out the window of his room, enthralled by a majestic mountain range or a lush garden valley. Wildflowers, birds, mountain streams, and soft breezes attracted him. The images John used in his writing reflect his devotion to nature.

However, John was not a romantic who viewed nature itself as God. John referred to the "nothingness" of the natural world. This was his way of saying that mountains, woods, and streams were totally dependent on God's sustaining love. Apart from this love, nature was "nothing." Meadows covered with flowers and a beautiful dawn embodied God's love. Thus, an experience of natural beauty draws our heart to God with joy.

For John, nature must be approached with an open heart and alive senses. To see nature as merely something to be used or exploited denies the grandeur of God's creative power. John's vision has special significance as humanity seeks to cherish the natural world as a gift from God.

✧ John once told his friars, "'To-day each one is to go alone through the mountains and spend the day in solitary prayer and in speaking to our Lord from his heart'" (Crisógono, *Life*, p. 196). Take John's advice. Find a place of natural beauty where you can spend the day, an hour, or even a few moments speaking with God.

✧ Read the "About John" section of this meditation again. Then recall a natural setting that had the power to draw you into a mood of solitude. Relax yourself; allow your breathing to become slow and rhythmic. By memory and imagination put yourself back into this setting. Allow your senses to work—smell, touch, listen, even taste, and rest there for as long as you like. God is with you there; invite the Creator to be with you.

✧ Slowly pray John's poem in the "John's Words" section. Continue this prayer by writing a list of natural images that have attracted your attention recently whether by their bright colors, soothing fragrance, cheery sound, or intriguing feel. Concentrate on a few of the more powerful images, and, if you feel the inclination, let them take the form of a drawing, a poem, or a journal excerpt.

✧ If you enjoy seeing through the eye of a camera, shoot a roll of film in a landscape that attracts you. Have one of these pictures enlarged and place it where it will remind you of the mystery of the natural world and God's nearness.

✧ Find an insignificant natural object—a stone, leaf, or twig—and simply gaze at it with all your attention and with faith that God's presence shines through it. When distractions occur (for instance, the thought "I could be doing something more important"), let them pass through your mind and return to the object. Practice this meditative seeing several times, and after each time, write a brief reflection or prayer on what you are seeing.

✧ For an examen of consciousness, pray with this question: How can I take even a few moments during each day to pray with nature?

God's Word

When daylight came [Jesus] left the house and made his way to a lonely place. (Luke 4:42)

Now it happened in those days that he went onto the mountain to pray; and he spent the whole night in prayer to God. (Luke 6:12)

Closing prayer: Slowly read John's expression of his love for God:

My beloved, the mountains
and lonely wooded valleys,
Strange islands,
And resounding rivers,
The whistling of love-stirring breezes,

The tranquil night
At the time of the rising dawn,
Silent music,
Sounding solitude,
The supper that refreshes, and deepens love.

      (John of the Cross, "The Spiritual Canticle")

The Blessings of Humor and Song

Theme: John laughed and sang because he trusted in God's love.

Opening prayer: I pray for the grace to celebrate through laughter and song.

About John

Whenever the nuns or friars under his care were sad, John shared his good cheer. He made sure that the friars had opportunities to relax, go for walks, and enjoy themselves. On long journeys, he liked to compose songs to make good use of the time.

John would try anything to entertain those who were sick. On one occasion he returned to the monastery to find all of the friars ill.

> The first step he took was to send for a joint of meat. He had it dressed and cooked and himself served it to the sick, encouraged them to eat, and, if necessary, ordered them to do so. At times he spoke to them of spiritual things, at other times of ordinary matters or of things to entertain them. The patients even heard him tell amusing stories. (Crisógono, *Life,* p. 149)

Pause: Reflect on your own sense of playfulness and your willingness to share it with other people.

John's Words

John's lighthearted song celebrated the created world and God's love.

> Let us rejoice, beloved,
> And let us go forth to behold ourselves in your beauty,
> To the mountain and to the hill,
> To where the pure water flows,
> And further, deep into the thicket.
>
> . . . .
>
> The breathing of the air,
> The song of the sweet nightingale
> The grove and its living beauty
> In the serene night,
> With a flame that is consuming and painless.
> (John of the Cross, "The Spiritual Canticle")

Reflection

To John, humor and song expressed a free and loving spirit, not a nervous and insecure one. Someone who can spontaneously laugh and sing from the sheer joy of living accepts and celebrates God's love. Sometimes when we take ourselves too seriously and give our life undue importance, we need humor and song to free us from ourselves. These characteristics can also reflect the deep inner calmness of an integrated person.

Besides, as John indicates, humor and song can be a balm to people in need. It can dissolve barriers of mistrust, connect people in surprising ways, and offer opportunities for people to help one another.

✧ Dance (no matter how ineptly), walk in the woods, sing a favorite song, or practice smiling as a form of meditation.

✧ Examine the following questions. You may want to write down your responses and reflections.

✦ When was the last time you tried to cheer a person who was sick or burdened with problems?

✦ What difficulties did you experience?

✦ How do you think you helped the person?

✦ How did that person feel afterward? How did you feel?

Go visit someone shut-in or ill. Bring flowers, a funny card, a treat, a story, or a joke. Maybe just hold the person's hand or listen respectfully.

✧ Looking at the world in which you live, do you think God has a sense of humor? If so, how is it expressed? And, thinking about the stories in the Bible, do you think Jesus was ever lighthearted and broke into laughter?

✧ List the sources of humor and song in your life, and then offer a prayer of gratitude for all the times you have enjoyed these riches.

✧ Recall a joyful spiritual experience that was, perhaps, filled with humor and song. Meditate on how you felt and how God was present to you at this time.

✧ What childlike quality would you like to cultivate in your personality? Children see joy in the commonplace things of life. What everyday, common events have you enjoyed today? Meditate on the small things that bring a smile to your face. List them and use them as a litany, repeating the phrase "Thank you, God" as you pray them.

✧ Offer a prayer for all those who are overwhelmed by depression.

God's Word

Sing out your joy to the Creator, good people;
for praise is fitting for loyal hearts.
Give thanks to the Creator upon the harp,
with a ten-stringed lute sing songs.
O sing a new song;
play skillfully and loudly so all may hear.
For the word of the Creator is faithful,
and all God's works are to be trusted.
The Creator loves justice and right
and fills the earth with faithful love.

(Psalm 33:1–5)

Closing prayer: Holy Friend, life is filled with your gifts to celebrate. I offer you this song in joy for your great love. (Sing a favorite hymn.)

✧ **Meditation 6** ✧

Hunger for Solitude

Theme: Solitude nourishes the spirit and gives it the opportunity to rest in God's love.

Opening prayer: Loving God, draw me aside so that I can be alone with you at the center of my being.

About John

Throughout his life, John hungered for quiet times to be alone with God. His deep love for silence and solitude brought him to the doors of the Carmelite order.

Even with his busy schedule, John found time for solitude. During a stay in Lisbon, he went off alone, Bible in hand, and walked along the seashore. Facing the expanse of the Atlantic, he read and meditated.

Just before the end of his life, John's opposition to some of the decisions of the new vicar general led to his de facto exile to the solitude of a monastery in La Peñuela in the region of Andalusia. Rather than rebel at his rejection, John gladly left his former activities and immersed himself in the welcome silence of the place.

> Every day on those delightful early mornings of summer on the Sierra Morena, he was up before daybreak. He went out . . . among some willow trees by a duct of

running water, knelt down and made his morning prayer. There he stayed until the heat of the sun forced him to return to the monastery. (Crisógono, *Life*, p. 282)

Even after reluctantly making plans to leave the monastery to have a serious infection treated, John wrote to a friend, "'I intend, however, to return here as quickly as possible, for it is certain that I am very well in this solitude'" (Crisógono, *Life*, p. 288).

Pause: Relax yourself by repeating a favorite prayer word. Be alone with God.

John's Words

Mountains have heights and they are affluent, vast, beautiful, graceful, bright and fragrant. These mountains are what my Beloved is to me. . . . Lonely valleys are quiet, pleasant, cool, shady, and flowing with fresh waters; in the variety of their groves and in the sweet song of the birds, they afford abundant recreation and delight to the senses, and in their solitude and silence they refresh and give rest. These valleys are what my Beloved is to me. (John of the Cross, "The Spiritual Canticle")

She lived in solitude,
And now in solitude has built her nest;
And in solitude he guides her,
He alone, who also bears
In solitude the wound of love.
        (John of the Cross, "The Spiritual Canticle")

Reflection

Like John the Baptist, on whose feast day he was born, John of the Cross longed for times of desert solitude and uninterrupted silence in which he could devote himself to uniting his spirit with God through prayer and contemplation. He wanted to make God's reality the center of his existence.

For this reason, he sought both external and internal silence to listen to God's promptings in his heart. He sometimes found this silence by rising in the stillness of the night and remaining alert to the presence of God's love. Contemplative life aided John's search for solitude, but all Christians need some time of aloneness and silence to listen to God and to align their will with that of God.

✧ Have you ever realized that talking, working, or interacting with others in your daily world was somehow not enough—that you needed some time alone? Write a description of this feeling.

✧ Spend fifteen minutes in silent attentiveness opening yourself to God's spirit. Allow distractions to pass through your mind without holding on to them. Simply and gently bring yourself back into God's presence. If an issue keeps floating through, maybe you are being invited to spend time talking to God about it.

✧ Time in solitude does not remove the responsibilities of daily life. Yet spending time in solitude allows us to reach a center of love, and that love can overflow into other activities.
+ When have you felt most frustrated or anxious, most overwhelmed with life experiences?
+ How could spending time alone in God's presence change your perspective on these experiences?

✧ In solitude, we have a good chance to face the truth about our self. Use your memory to answer these questions: Have there been times when I have tried to avoid solitude? If so, when and why? What are my favorite distractions or avoidance techniques?
Talk with God about a part of your life that you try to keep hidden. Ask God to give you the grace to enter your own aloneness.

✧ Find a space for solitude and silence. Read passages from the Bible that have importance for you. Let the words fill the silence and enter your heart. Respond to the reading by

talking with God, and if you feel the words fall away, simply rest in God's presence.

✧ Pray the section "John's Words" repeatedly and slowly. Offer each word like a precious gift to God.

God's Word

"But when you pray, go to your private room, shut yourself in, and so pray . . . in that secret place, and your [God] who sees all that is done in secret will reward you." (Matthew 6:6)

Closing prayer: I approach you, O God, in the depths of my aloneness, and ask you to fill my silence with your love and with a deeper faith.

☩ Meditation 7   ✧

Soul Friendship

Theme: Soul friends play an integral role in our growth to love God. What we love in another person is the vibrant, mysterious, still-center that is given to them by God.

Opening prayer: Thank you, gracious God, for the friends that you have brought into my life.

About John

Two of John's closest friends were his brother, Francisco, and Teresa of Ávila.

Francisco often accompanied John as he preached in neighboring villages, and Francisco stayed with John at the monasteries in Duruelo, Granada, and Segovia. Francisco was well known for his humility and good works. Some people wondered whether John would ever be as holy as his brother. John delighted in his brother, and when people came to visit him, he was quick to introduce Francisco, saying, "'May I introduce you to my brother, who is the treasure I most value in the world'" (Crisógono, *Life*, p. 211).

When John met Teresa for the first time, they felt an immediate rapport. At Teresa's request, John became confessor at the Convent of the Incarnation, where they worked together harmoniously. But even when they disagreed, their deep friendship remained intact. During this time together, Teresa arrived at an extraordinary state of union with God. In a letter recalling John's time with her at Ávila, Teresa declared:

> "I can tell you, daughter, that since he went away I have found no one like him in all Castile nor anyone who inspires people with so much fervour on the way to heaven. You would not believe how solitary his absence makes me feel. . . .
>   . . . he is indeed the father of my soul." (Crisógono, *Life*, p. 132)

Likewise, John was deeply saddened when he was unable to see Teresa. After her death, he kept a portrait of her with him wherever he went. Her image nurtured his inner peace and encouraged him. This picture was one of the last things he relinquished.

Pause: Ask yourself: Who is the soul friend that nurtures my spirit?

John's Words

Toward the end of his life, when two friars began trying to build a case against John to have him dismissed from the Carmelites, many of his correspondents burned their letters from John in an attempt to protect their friend. As a result, only a few of his letters remain. Nevertheless, one of his letters to a friend reveals John's quiet but deep affection:

> "Jesus be in your soul. A few days ago I wrote to you through Padre Fray Juan in answer to your last letter, which, as was your hope, I prized. I have answered you in that letter, since I believe I have received all your letters. And I have felt your grief, afflictions, and loneliness. These, in silence, ever tell me so much that the pen cannot declare it." (Hardy, *Search for Nothing*, p. 140)

Reflection

Though John warned that we should not love one person more than another on our journey toward greater detachment, obviously he himself had preferences. Is this a contradiction?

His advice was not meant to be an end in itself, but as a warning against restrictive or harmful relationships that might slow the spiritual journey. Once a person learns what self-sacrifice means, the need for John's warning becomes less necessary because the heart is more open to authentic love from all sources. John knew from his own friendships that people are drawn to certain others because of their unique personalities and sensitivities.

According to John, we should determine the truth of our relationships by evaluating whether the other person draws us to God or takes us away from God. Good friendships enhance our spiritual growth, rather than hinder it.

✧ Write a letter to a close friend expressing your care and friendship—or plan to visit a friend you have wanted to see but, due to time or circumstances, have been unable to.

✧ Who was the first person interested in the real you, the person who opened the door to deeper levels of yourself? Reflect on the impact this person had on your life. Repeat the person's name in prayer as an offering of thanksgiving to God.

✧ To understand the importance of John's warning against attachments to harmful relationships, recall a relationship that you became involved in for the wrong reasons and that adversely affected your spiritual development. Talk to Jesus about this relationship.

✧ Recall a time when you were hurt by a close friend. Were the two of you able to heal the hurt and become reconciled? How did this hurt affect your spirituality?

✧ Without worrying about artistic merit, draw a picture or symbol of a dear friend. Ponder the goodness this person represents to you, and the love you experience through her or him. List the ways this person has been a gift to you. Thank God for your good friend.

✧ List people to whom you have been a soul friend or a dependable, caring friend. Next to each name, briefly describe what positive qualities of yours this relationship has drawn out of you. For instance, if you have been a good friend to an elderly person, maybe you have learned that you are more patient than you thought. Thank God for these friends and the gifts you have recognized because of them.

✧ Recount a story that reveals your affection for a brother or a sister. Think about the history of this relationship and the role that this person plays in your life.

God's Word

Two are better than one, because they have a good reward for their toil. For if they fall, one will lift up the other; but woe to one who is alone and falls and does not have another to help. Again, if two lie together, they keep warm; but how can one keep warm alone? And though one might prevail against another, two will withstand one. A threefold cord is not quickly broken. (Ecclesiastes 4:9–12, NRSV)

Closing prayer: Loving God, give me the grace to stay true to the friendships I receive from you, and allow them to take root in your grace and to blossom.

Gentle Care of Souls

Theme: As John's intimate love for God grew, people sought spiritual direction from him. This same love enabled John to be an encouraging and empathetic spiritual companion.

Opening prayer: Grant me, O God, wisdom, understanding, and love to nurture the spiritual welfare of my sisters and brothers. May I be a gentle companion for their journey.

About John

Whenever John was transferred to a new convent or monastery, his reputation as a confessor and spiritual guide spread quickly. He directed not only the learned but also simple people, both religious and lay. John avoided giving harsh penance that was customary in his time, and instead concentrated on the spiritual needs of each person.

Recognizing the importance of every meeting, John was patient with those who came to him and refused to rush through their time together. He gave not only spiritual advice but material help as well. If he noticed that someone was without means, he gave them money from monastery funds. He had a gift for finding just the right words to help each person he met. For example:

One day, Sister Catalina de la Cruz, the cook, a candid and simple soul, asked him why when she went near a pool of water they had in the garden, the frogs that were on the brink leapt into the water almost before they could hear the sound of her footsteps and hid themselves in the depths of the pool. Fray John told her it was because that was the place and centre where they were in security. . . . "That is what you must do," he said to her; "flee from creatures and plunge into the depth and centre, which is God, hiding yourself in him." (Crisógono, *Life*, p. 134)

John wanted to understand the experience of people who sought his counsel. So he asked them about themselves and then listened respectfully. One day he asked this question of Francisca de la Madre de Dios:

"In what does prayer consist?" . . . "In looking at the beauty of God and rejoicing that he has it," replied the nun. Fray John [was] delighted with this thought. (Crisógono, *Life*, p. 134)

As an empathetic spiritual companion, John could delight in someone else's gifts and insights.

Pause: Reflect on the way John accepted and delighted in Francisca's response to his question.

John's Words

When he was a young priest stationed at Teresa of Ávila's Convent of the Incarnation, John was approached by a young nun who thought that due to John's growing reputation as a holy man, he would be a demanding and unsympathetic spiritual director. John calmed her:

A confessor who is holy ought not to frighten people. "I . . . am not so, but the holier the confessor the gentler he is and the less he is scandalized at other people's faults, because he understands man's weak condition better." (Crisógono, *Life*, p. 75)

Reflection

Though he demanded much from himself, John showed gentleness and kindness in his direction of others. His quiet and compassionate manner may have been taken as a sign of passivity at first, but those who were counseled by him discovered his uncommon spiritual wisdom and great heart. The best spiritual directors, like John, start by listening. Then they listen some more, trying to understand other people by walking around in their shoes. Only with this kind of understanding can a spiritual director provide helpful counsel.

In his writings, John often warns about spiritual directors who attempt to advise others, but only pass along their own ignorance. These individuals, he says, can cause serious harm by holding back or waylaying spiritual growth.

We may not consider ourselves spiritual directors, but each of us has a unique ability to spread God's word to others. This apostolate takes many forms, depending on our way of life and our abilities. John helps us recognize our responsibility to encourage the spiritual growth of others in a gentle and compassionate manner, using empathetic listening and honoring the dignity and uniqueness of each person's spiritual path.

✧ Reread John's comment to the young nun who came to see him. Meditate on his conviction that true holiness brings with it the gentle understanding of human weakness. Do you believe this? Do you accept and understand your own weakness? Are you gentle with other people's weakness?

✧ Recall recent instances when someone has come to talk to you about an important matter. Ask yourself: Do I listen to other people with humility and respect when they share their inner life with me? Am I too quick to interject my suggestions and views? Ask God for the graces you need to be an empathetic listener like John.

✧ Recall a time when you encouraged, took delight in, or supported someone on their spiritual journey. You may not have given advice, but somehow you showed that person the importance of her or his spiritual experience.

✦ What did you do?
✦ What was the response of the other person?
✦ How did you feel about the encounter?
Pray for this person for whom, even if briefly, you were a spiritual companion.

✧ Ponder the ways you can be a more active and empathetic spiritual companion to your family, co-workers, friends, or congregants at your church. Maybe the ways include listening better, being physically present, offering advice, or sharing your own story. Can you think of other ways?

✧ Relax your body and mind by stretching your muscles, breathing deeply, and sitting quietly. When you are ready, recall key people who have been your spiritual companions, mentors who have nourished your spirit on its journey. Recount all their acts and words that have been important to you. Finally, pray for each one, lifting them up to God.

God's Word

"Come to me, all you who labour and are overburdened, and I will give you rest. Shoulder my yoke and learn from me, for I am gentle and humble in heart, and you will find rest for your souls. Yes, my yoke is easy and my burden light." (Matthew 11:28–30)

Closing prayer: Gentle God, teach me to listen, and then give me the courage and wisdom to offer your love to others in a way that is most suited to them. Let me share my hunger for you with gentleness and compassion.

✧ Meditation 9 ✧

Poetry and Prayer

Theme: The experience of God's love can be expressed through images that rise from the center of the heart. For John, writing poems gave life to these images.

Opening prayer: Awaken me, mysterious Spirit, to the images that spring from the depths of my soul.

About John

Poetic images and rhythms surfaced spontaneously in John's life as an expression of his love for God and Mary. During his novitiate, John composed songs in different verse styles as an expression of deep gratitude for the Carmelite way of life he had chosen.

However, the most dramatic outpouring of poetic images occurred during his imprisonment. At first, John had no writing utensils with which to record his inner experiences. Indeed, his captors flogged, starved, and tried to break him with solitary confinement. But then a young priest was assigned guard responsibilities and, recognizing the holiness of his prisoner, pitied John. He brought John clean clothing to replace the rags he was wearing, and provided the paper and ink John requested.

The young warder brought them and Fray John, taking advantage of the short time when the light of noonday came into the slot which was no more than three fingers wide, wrote lyric poems . . . which he had been mentally composing in the solitude of his prison. . . .

The lyric poems, all, that is, except the *romances,* reflect his state of imprisonment: images of sorrow, laments, persistent imagery of night and darkness. (Crisógono, *Life,* p. 108)

John used his poems to inspire others to seek the light of God's love. One nun, perceiving the beauty and profound meaning of his images, asked John if he had been inspired by God. "'Daughter,' he replied, 'sometimes they came to me from God and at other times I sought them.'" (Crisógono, *Life,* p. 138).

Pause: What images consistently bubble up from the depths of your own unconscious when you recall God's love?

John's Words

Responding to the request of the prioress of the Carmelite nuns in Granada to comment on stanzas of "The Spiritual Canticle," John wrote:

"I do not plan to expound these stanzas in all the breadth and fullness that the fruitful spirit of love conveys to them. It would be foolish to think that expressions of love arising from mystical understanding, like these stanzas, are fully explainable. . . .

Who can describe the understanding He gives to loving souls in whom He dwells? And who can express the experience He imparts to them? Who, finally, can explain the desires he gives them? Certainly, no one can! Not even they who receive these communications. As a result these persons let something of their experiences overflow in figures and similes, and from the abundance of their spirit pour out secrets and mysteries rather than rational explanations."

(John of the Cross, "The Spiritual Canticle")

Reflection

The images that overflow from John's love of God reveal the inner geography of his soul—the dark night, the absent lover, marriage, mountains, flowers, gardens, woods, thickets, shepherds, silent music, the wounded soul, riverbanks, birds, lions. They are not simply expressions of his personality, but reflections of the deep current of his selfless love for God.

Primary images emerge from our own relationship with God. John suggests we pay attention to these images because they tell the story of our spiritual journey. To ignore them and instead depend on rational explanations as a way of uncovering spiritual depths is like trying to draw water from a dry well. The mystery of the human spirit reveals itself best in the primary human expression of images. On this level, we discover our own ineffable spiritual adventure.

✧ Take time to rest in silence and focus on the presence of God's love in your life. Use a concrete image or images that represent this love for you—a garden, the sea, a mountain, or a flower—and allow your imagination to give life to the image. Experience sounds, tastes, textures, smells, and sights. Let the feelings that surround this image rise up within you and draw you to an even deeper love for God.

✧ List images from the Bible, poetry, or your own imagination that have caught your attention and resonate deeply for you. Go through the list and let yourself experience the attraction of each image in turn. Write a prayer using these images.

✧ Write a psalm—which means "song"—that pours out your feelings right now. Like the psalmists, hold nothing back: anger, sorrow, joy, or thanksgiving. God already knows what is in your heart anyway. Writing out your feelings helps you share who you are with God, your holy and true friend.

✧ One helpful way of expressing an image that strikes to the soul of our experience is to write haiku. The traditional Japanese haiku have a specific number and pattern of syllables, with the central purpose of capturing an image to see it in a new way. In English, haiku are often written in three lines. Here are two examples.

> A black bear pawing
> Fast-moving gray clouds, thunder
> Storms the apple tree

> The beagle's wet nose
> reminds me
> my child is coming out to play.

Write your own haiku. Creation itself and the experience of creation magnify God's work. Look at what is around you here and now that speaks of God's goodness to you. Write.

✧ Listen to or play a piece of music that lifts your soul and fills it with images of God's grandeur. Sing a favorite hymn in praise of God's great love.

God's Word

My love is mine and I am his.
He pastures his flock among the lilies.

Before the day-breeze rises,
before the shadows flee,
return! Be, my love,
like a gazelle, like a young stag,
on the mountains of Bether.

On my bed, at night, I sought
the man who is my sweetheart:
I sought but could not find him!
So I shall get up and go through the city;
in the streets and in the squares,
I shall seek my sweetheart.
I sought but could not find him!

(The Song of Songs 2:16—3:2)

Closing prayer: Holy Spirit, unlock my heart and let my love flow freely with images that express my deepest yearning. I sing with John,

How gently and lovingly
You wake in my heart,
Where in secret you dwell alone;
And in your sweet breathing,
Filled with good and glory,
How tenderly you swell my heart with love.

(John of the Cross, "The Living Flame of Love")

✧ **Meditation 10** ✧

Entering the Dark Night

Theme: When we answer the divine call to love, the spirit of God invites us into a dark night where we are stripped of our attachments and compulsions. As a result, we are drawn closer to God.

Opening prayer: O God, burn away my limitations and my selfishness. Call me to transformation even if I must first be plunged into darkness.

About John

When John's captors threw him into a tiny cell, John experienced his own intense dark night of the soul and senses.

> The first minutes in this cell, as his eyes adjusted to the darkness, were terrifying. He stumbled across something on the floor. Gradually his eyes could see more in the darkness and with his fingers he found what was to be his bed: a couple of boards on the floor and an old blanket or two to protect himself just a bit from the wintry dampness of the cold stone floors and walls. A bucket sat in the corner. This was to be his toilet. . . . This dark and smelly place was to be his home for several more months. In fact it was to be a place of both physical and spiritual darkness, anguish, and pain. (P. 66)

. . . He suffered the complete absence of God. It was not just a light, momentary absence, such as most believers know from experience. It was total. All his life, past and present, seemed to him to be wasted. He could no longer pray. The very thought of God made him sick, even physically sick. He felt abandoned in his degradation. . . . He who was so meticulous about personal cleanliness had not been able to wash for months. The summer heat was beginning: a stifling, unbearable, scorching heat. His closet cell was an oven. (Hardy, *Search for Nothing*, p. 70)

Pause: Recall a time when you felt God's absence in your own life. Think of your struggle, the questions you asked, and the physical and spiritual torment you underwent.

John's Words

After his escape from prison, John tried to explain the purifying nature of his dark night.

A deeper enlightenment and wider experience than mine is necessary to explain the dark night through which a soul journeys toward that divine light of perfect union with God that is achieved, insofar as possible in this life, through love. The darknesses and trials, spiritual and temporal, that fortunate souls ordinarily undergo on their way to the high state of perfection are so numerous and profound that human science cannot understand them adequately. Nor does experience of them equip one to explain them. Those who suffer them will know what this experience is like, but they will find themselves unable to describe it.

. . . Indeed, it is a period for leaving these persons alone in the purgation God is working in them, a time to give comfort and encouragement that they may desire to endure this suffering as long as God wills, for until then, no remedy—whatever the soul does, or the confessor says—is adequate. (John of the Cross, "The Ascent of Mount Carmel")

John used images in his poetry to illustrate the ascent from the dark night.

> A song of the soul's happiness in having passed through the dark night of faith, in nakedness and purgation, to union with its Beloved.

> One dark night,
> Fired with love's urgent longings
> —Ah, the sheer grace!—
> I went out unseen,
> My house being now all stilled;
>
> . . . .
>
> On that glad night,
> In secret, for no one saw me,
> Nor did I look at anything,
> With no other light or guide
> Than the one that burned in my heart;
>
> This guided me
> More surely than the light of noon
> To where he waited for me
> —him I knew so well—
> In a place where no one appeared.
> (John of the Cross, "The Ascent of Mount Carmel")

Reflection

John uses darkness to describe all the stages of the spiritual journey. He emphasizes that darkness is not our own doing, but a state brought about by God that weans us from our attachments and compulsions. John refers to two kinds of darkness. One cleanses the senses in order to bring them into harmony with the spirit. This is darkness for beginners, and it introduces them to contemplation. The other darkness is more difficult. It affects the spirit and prepares it for union with God.

At the beginning of the spiritual journey, we enter into darkness by letting go of attachments. For instance, in a time of crisis, old answers and all of our possessions are inadequate explanations or compensations for the turmoil or loss we feel. In our distress, we detach ourselves from these things that had been our security and turn to God. We are pilgrims starting the spiritual journey feeling joy in God's presence and in prayer but then suddenly entering a night where there is no pleasure in God or the world. Meditation becomes difficult and no longer seems helpful. The desire to move toward God is frustrated. In this darkness, we learn to cry out to the one source of help—God. In the process, we learn to live in darkness through grace, and we find that God alone is sufficient.

William Johnston says that in the darkness, the soul exclaims:

"God was present all the time and I did not recognize Him. I thought it was darkness but it was light. I thought it was nothing but it was all." . . . As excessive light of the sun blinds the human eye, so the excessive light of God plunges man into thick darkness.

And God is approached in darkness and emptiness and nothingness simply because He is the mystery of mysteries." (*The Inner Eye of Love: Mysticism and Religion*, pp. 121–122)

Not everyone is plunged into a continuous state of darkness, says John. Most people experience it intermittently. In any case, John learned to accept darkness not as a curse, but as a gift. He knew that attempts to avoid darkness through distractions, rationalizations, anger, or pleasure would only lead to disillusionment and dissipation. God, the ultimate light, dwells in and calls to us from the darkness.

✧ Bring to mind times when you felt the dark night of the senses—during intense physical suffering; when you had to let go of your own concerns in order to reach out to someone else; when you denied yourself a particular pleasure not because you thought it was wrong but because you felt the need to experience a greater love; when your own efforts collapsed and you had to rely on God. See yourself during these times. Where were you? What were you doing? What did you think about? And then ask yourself: What did I learn from these experiences? To what transformation of spirit was God calling me? How did I answer?

✧ Recall a time when you felt a dark night of the soul—a point at which you felt adrift in a sea of confusion and meaninglessness, alone, abandoned by God. Did you try to escape from the dark night? If so, how? Did you somehow encounter God in a new way during this time?

✧ Is there some issue or relationship that is leading you into darkness, frustration, or feelings of abandonment right now? Is God trying to free you from an unhealthy attachment or from clinging to an illusion? Call on the Holy Spirit to be with you, and offer "the living flame of love" your feelings and concerns.

✧ Take a walk at night. Or play music that evokes the mood of nightfall, such as Chopin's "Nocturnes." Or draw images of night. Or sit quietly in a darkened room. Then, breathing deeply with your eyes closed, rest silently in the presence of God. If some concern disturbs you, let it go by focusing on breathing gently. Invite the spirit of God into your soul.

✧ In the spiritual night, we allow God to act in our life. But, can you remember times when you have wanted to take control of your spirituality, to direct God's action rather than let God transform your soul? Reflect on the result of your efforts.

✧ Entering the darkness means responding to the transforming power of God's love. Ask God for help in accepting the changes in your life.

✧ To experience this darkness is also to experience the need for contemplation.
+ Have you felt drawn to solitude and silence where you can rest in God's presence?
+ Have you obeyed this call or have you allowed it to be masked by your busy schedule?

✦ Take time now to breathe deeply, relax, and concentrate on God's love. Use prayer words like *love* or *merciful God* to refocus your attention when you become distracted. The mantra should be a word or phrase that has spiritual power for you.

God's Word

Then Jesus came with them to a plot of land called Gethsemane; and he said to his disciples, "Stay here while I go over there to pray." He took Peter and the two sons of Zebedee with him. And he began to feel sadness and anguish.

Then he said to them, "My soul is sorrowful to the point of death. . . ." And going on a little further he fell on his face and prayed. "My Father," he said, "if it is possible, let this cup pass me by. Nevertheless, let it be as you, not I, would have it." He came back to the disciples and found them sleeping, and he said to Peter, "So you had not the strength to stay awake with me for one hour? Stay awake, and pray not to be put to the test. The spirit is willing enough, but human nature is weak." Again, a second time, he went away and prayed: "My Father," he said, "if this cup cannot pass by, but I must drink it, your will be done!" (Matthew 26:36–42)

Closing prayer: While reading the following stanza from John's "The Ascent of Mount Carmel," recall the love that fills the darkness and draws you toward transformation.

O guiding night!
O night more lovely than the dawn!
O night that has united
The lover with his beloved,
Transforming the beloved in her lover.
  (John of the Cross, "The Ascent of Mount Carmel")

✧ Meditation 11 ✧

Freeing the Heart

Theme: John understood that the heart must be free from inordinate attachments in order to respond to the love of God.

Opening prayer: Give me the courage and strength to participate in the transformation you have begun in my life, loving and gentle God.

About John

When John acted as a spiritual director to the nuns at Beas, he spoke about the practice of detachment. Some nuns copied down this discourse, which later was found almost word for word in his work, "The Ascent of Mount Carmel."

[His advice] for overcoming the appetites: "Have a general desire of imitating Jesus Christ in all his works, in conformity with his life, about which we must think in order to know how to imitate it and behave in all things as he would have done. In order to be able to do this, it is necessary to renounce any appetite or taste which is not purely for the glory of God and remain in a kind of void for love of him who in this life had no more and wanted no more than to do the will of his Father." (Crisógono, *Life*, p. 135)

One day he gave the nuns a sketch of Mount Carmel, which represented a summary of his teaching on detachment. The mountain had three dark lines that represented paths to the top. The two side paths were detours, the middle one was the path of perfection. The middle path invited the spirit to reject all desires so nothing would make it weary and divert it from its goal of God alone. Below the mountain was a series of *"nadas"* that directed the spiritual journey:

> To reach satisfaction in all
> desire its possession in nothing.
> To come to possess all
> desire the possession of nothing.
> To arrive at being all
> desire to be nothing.
> To come to the knowledge of all
> desire the knowledge of nothing.

> . . . .

> To come to be what you are not
> you must go by a way in which you are not.
> When you turn toward something
> you cease to cast yourself upon the all.
> For to go from all to the all
> you must deny yourself of all in all.
> And when you come to the possession of the all
> you must possess it without wanting anything.
> Because if you desire to have something in all
> your treasure in God is not purely your all.
> (John of the Cross, "The Ascent of Mount Carmel")

John realized that his advice sounded harsh, so he left behind a copy of his poems for the nuns, hoping they would realize that detachment is impossible unless they were passionately answering the call of God's transforming love as it was offered to them in their daily life. Besides, he knew that the *"nada,"* or nothing, was filled with God.

Pause: Reflect on this question: What persons, things, or habits have I become so attached to in my life that they are hindering my ability to love God and my neighbor?

John's Words

A ray of sunlight shining on a smudgy window is unable to illumine that window completely and transform it into its own light. It could do this if the window were cleaned and polished. The less the film and stain are wiped away, the less the window will be illumined; and the cleaner the window is, the brighter will be its illumination. . . .

The soul on which the divine light of God's being is ever shining, or better, in which it is ever dwelling by nature, is like this window. . . .

A soul makes room for God by wiping away all the smudges. . . . When this is done the soul will be illumined by and transformed in God. (John of the Cross, "The Ascent of Mount Carmel")

Reflection

John tells us that spiritual growth begins with rejecting the attachments in our life that control us. We can enjoy food and be attracted to it, but eating indiscriminately or compulsively will hinder our spiritual journey. We should enjoy relationships with others, but if love turns to control or manipulation for our own purposes then we forfeit our inner peace and destroy love. As William Johnston says, "This nothingness [that John writes about] is not the renunciation of all things, but, the renunciation of clinging to all things—and it is done in order that I may love these same things truly, as they are in themselves, without projections" (*The Inner Eye,* p. 123).

John knew that our desires and affections must be reordered toward God if we are to encounter God in our life. In answering the invitation of love, we open the door of our heart by removing obstacles and entering to meet God. Forcing ourselves to let go of attachments can actually increase our desire for the attachment. So John suggests that we simply respond to God's invitation to let go as it occurs in our unique history. Each day we are asked to die to ourselves in unexpected ways—listening to someone when we would rather be doing other things, assuming a responsibility we never asked for, experiencing rejection, facing our limitations, and so on.

We may think that we are seeking God, says John, but God is seeking us much more than we realize. Our own love and release of attachments is actually a response to God loving us first. After all, Jesus' own path involved accepting the cross because of the love of God. In responding to this love, John of the Cross reminds us of the words of John the Evangelist, "Only by dying to ourselves can we find ourselves" (Adapted from John 12:25).

✧ Slowly read John's list of *"nadas"* in the "About John" section of this meditation. As you read this, ponder how each *"nada"* applies to you.

✧ John warns us that seemingly insignificant attachments that become habitual have the power to enslave the heart. John used the image of a small thread holding a bird captive. Reflect on the following questions:

✦ Do I find myself regularly wanting to attract attention to myself?
✦ Do I have favorite possessions that I find difficult to sacrifice, even in the face of someone else's desperate need?
✦ Are there tasks that I perform that I feel no one else could possibly handle properly?
✦ Am I quite particular about the way food is prepared or the way it tastes?

✧ Choose an attachment that has begun to take hold of your heart and consider the power it has over you. How do you feel about this attachment? What is God asking from you in this case?

✧ Reread John's talk to the nuns of Beas in the "About John" section and reflect on his suggestion that we can free ourselves from enslavement to our desires by imitating Christ.

✦ Choose a passage from the Gospels that has a special meaning for you.
✦ Read the passage closely and prayerfully.

✦ Ask yourself how God may be asking you to change your life, and why you may be avoiding this invitation.

✦ Set aside time on a regular basis to read the Gospels and to reflect on Christ's life.

✧ Think of people you know or have read about who craved something or someone to fill the emptiness of their life. Think about the suffering they experienced themselves and the suffering they may have caused to the object of their craving. Now reflect on the suffering you may have endured by indiscriminately following one of your own desires. Did you inflict any pain on anyone else because of this desire?

God's Word

In everything we prove ourselves authentic servants of God; by resolute perseverance in times of hardships, difficulties and distress; . . . in patience, in kindness; in the Holy Spirit, in a love free of affectation; . . . taken for impostors and yet we are genuine; unknown and yet we are acknowledged; dying, and yet here we are, alive; . . . in pain yet always full of joy; poor and yet making many people rich; having nothing, and yet owning everything. (2 Corinthians 6:4–10)

Closing prayer: Gracious God, I join with John "and desire to enter for Christ into complete nudity, emptiness, and poverty in everything" (John of the Cross, "The Ascent of Mount Carmel"). Free my heart; liberate my will.

Embracing the Cross

Theme: The model of the spiritual way is Jesus Christ himself who suffered on the cross to reconcile all of humankind to God.

Opening prayer: Jesus, teach me to follow your path, to assume your receptivity, and to imitate your total fidelity to God's purpose.

About John

One of the favourite themes of his sermons to and conversations with the nuns was the value of suffering. He spoke from his very soul and could not conceal the fact. One day he had to go into the enclosure. Hanging on the wall of a certain cloister was a symbolic picture of the Passion of our Lord according to the allegory of the Prophet Isaias—Christ, like a bunch of grapes, was pouring forth his blood beneath the weight of the cross which was in the shape of the beam of a wine-press. Fray John stopped as he passed in front of it. He stood still looking at it and, with his face radiant, composed a poem on the impression the picture had made on him. Afterwards he put his arms around a great cross there was in the cloister, whilst fervently and deeply moved he uttered some words in Latin which the nuns did not understand. It was perhaps at this time that he repeated to them, . . . "Daughter, seek nothing but the bare cross, which is a lovely thing." (Crisógono, *Life*, p. 267)

Pause: Reflect on the meaning of Christ's cross in your own life, especially during your times of suffering.

John's Words

Our Lord proclaimed through St. Matthew: *My yoke is sweet and my burden (the cross) light* [Mt 11:30]. If individuals resolutely submit to the carrying of the cross, if they decidedly want to find and endure trial in all things for God, they will discover in all of them great relief and sweetness. This will be so because they will be traveling the road denuded of all and with no desire for anything. If they aim after the possession of something, from God or elsewhere, their journey will not be one of nakedness and detachment from all things, and consequently there will be no room for them on this narrow path nor will they be able to climb it. (John of the Cross, "The Ascent of Mount Carmel")

Reflection

John offers us the only spiritual way he knew—Jesus Christ. To understand John is to understand that we must surrender our self to God's will and empty our self of all attachments as Jesus Christ surrendered himself for us. John desired only to be empty of all things so that he could be filled with Christlife. To do so, he took Paul's words to the Philippians to heart:

Make your own the mind of Christ Jesus:

Who, being in the form of God,
did not count equality with God
something to be grasped.

> But he emptied himself,
> taking the form of a slave,
> becoming as human beings are;
>
> and being in every way like a human being,
> he was humbler yet,
> even to accepting death, death on a cross.
>
> And for this God raised him high.
>
> (2:5–9)

Jesus did not cling to his divinity or to his physical life. In the cross, John saw that Jesus opened his arms in love for all humanity and for God. The cross is the school in which Jesus teaches John and us freedom from attachments and the desire to do God's will.

John was not interested in some ideal state of perfection but in the continuous act of turning away from self to Christ. To the extent that we surrender in love to God we can make a place in our heart for the infinite love that God pours out through Jesus.

✧ John once had a vision of Christ on the cross and drew a rough sketch of what he saw. During times of recreation, he carved small crucifixes out of wood. Draw or carve your own image of Christ crucified, one that appeals to you or calls you to prayer.

✧ Meditate on the figure of Christ on a crucifix. Study Christ's figure from different angles, asking yourself: How is Christ speaking to me? Then meditate on this question: When Christ looked down from the cross, what did he see? What did he think?

✧ Think of suffering you have experienced and how this may have been an invitation to carry the cross of Christ. Write about one or two of these difficult times. Looking back at the event, do you see it differently now?

✧ Meditate on the "John's Words" section, concentrating on the "relief and sweetness" that results from freely taking on suffering that comes your way. What do you think John meant by this phrase?

✧ Reflect on Jesus' agony, horror, and shock as he was being led to his death. No angel came to save him; his followers abandoned him; he would hang with a murderer; and he had been unjustly accused. No one even offered to help carry the cross; a stranger was forced to do it. He was stripped naked and mocked. A heavy darkness fell, obliterating any sign of hope. His cry of desolation to Abba seemed fruitless. Only his faith and his total commitment to Abba, whose presence he no longer felt, sustained him.

✦ Compare this to a dark time in your own life, a time when you had to depend on faith alone.

✦ Focus on your own suffering and offer it to Christ to be transformed. How is your suffering freeing you from attachments or compulsions?

✧ Through the image of Christ crucified, John reminds us that love requires letting go of our self-centeredness and often involves suffering. List the people you have relationships with, for example, family members, co-workers, enemies, and friends. Next to each name, note the attachments you must let go of in order to improve and nurture love in this relationship. Recognize the way love has been calling you to let go of yourself. While contemplating Christ on the cross, pray for the grace necessary to open your arms in love.

God's Word

I have been crucified with Christ and yet I am alive; yet it is no longer I, but Christ living in me. The life that I am now living, subject to the limitation of human nature, I am living in faith, faith in the Son of God who loved me and gave himself for me. (Galatians 2:20–21)

Closing prayer: Jesus, live in me. Be with me as I take up my cross.

Devotion to Mary

Theme: Mary, the mother of the human and divine Jesus, shows that consenting love can bring about our transformation.

Opening prayer: Mary, teach me to live a selfless life, a life filled with the fire of love.

About John

When he was a child, John had a near-drowning experience in a well that sealed his devotion to Mary.

> All of a sudden he fell in, and the water reached up to his neck. He was nearly drowned, when a most beautiful lady appeared above him. . . . Mary lovingly said to him: "Give me your hand, child, and I will take you out." (Bruno, *St. John*, p. 4)

This vision of Mary dominated John's consciousness for the rest of his life and helped him choose the habit of the Carmelite Order.

Later, when John was in prison, the image of Mary enabled John to survive his ordeal. On the eve of the Feast of the Assumption, the prior who oversaw his punishment came to visit him. John was kneeling, bowed over, praying. The prior

asked John, "'What, then, were you thinking about just now?'
. . . 'That to-morrow is our Lady's feast and how much I
should love to say Mass,' replied Fray John. 'Not while I am
here,' answered [the prior] brusquely and went out, securing
the door behind him." (Crisógono, *Life*, p. 111)

Pause: Reflect on the role Mary plays in your own spiritual life.

John's Words

Then He summoned an archangel,
Saint Gabriel: and when he came,
Sent him forth to find a maiden,
    Mary was her name.

Only through her consenting love
Could the mystery be preferred
That the Trinity in human
    Flesh might clothe the Word.

Though the three Persons worked the wonder
It only happened in the One.
So was the Word made incarnation
    In Mary's womb, a son.

. . . .

By Mary, and with her own flesh
He was clothed in His own frame:
Both Son of God and Son of Man
    Together had one name.
        (John of the Cross, "Romance VIII")

Reflection

Throughout his life, John lived not only in the service of God,
but also in the service of Mary. Her image could be found
among the few objects that he cherished. It gave him light and
filled his heart with love.

John also saw Mary as a model of consenting love, or willing cooperation with the Divine Will. Mary accepted God's invitation so that the Incarnation could happen "in the One." She can teach us how to be obedient—that is, how to listen to God and how to love.

✧ Mary is often looked to as the protector of poor and downtrodden people. Indeed, she has consoled suffering Christians for centuries. Think of how Mary can be solace for poor and abused people. Then think of how she can be solace for those parts of you that need healing. Meditate on the "God's Word" section that follows.

✧ Recall the image of Mary that you had as a child; then draw a symbol representing Mary as you see her today.

✧ Mary's willingness to accept God's will should serve as an example in our own relationship with God. Write your thoughts on responding obediently to God's will in your life. Let your writing move from self-reflection to a conversation with Mary.

✧ Sing a favorite Marian hymn. As you sing, attend carefully to the words.

✧ Mary carried Jesus the Christ for nine months and then gave birth to him. Meditate on how you bear Christ and bring him to life in your relationships with other people.

God's Word

Pray with these words from "The Magnificat":

My being proclaims your greatness,
and my spirit finds joy in you, God my Savior.

For you have looked upon me, your servant, in my
lowliness;
all ages to come shall call me blessed.

God, you who are mighty, have done great things for me. Holy is your name.

Your mercy is from age to age toward those who fear you.
(Nancy Schreck and Maureen Leach, comps.,
Psalms Anew: In Inclusive Language, p. 16)

Closing prayer: Mary, mother of God, just as you brought Christ into the world, you bring me hope that my own life will be filled with truth and love.

Humility

Theme: Humility allows us to see and accept ourselves as we are, totally dependent on God's good graces.

Opening prayer:

May I accept my past,
May I accept my present,
May I accept my future,
May I have the wisdom and courage to humbly accept
    God's will in my history.

About John

Even as prior, John gladly took on jobs like washing dishes, serving at table, sweeping floors, or cleaning the latrines—jobs that his society viewed as undignified for a religious superior. Though he was held in great esteem for his knowledge of the Scriptures, his spiritual wisdom, and his ability to lead, John did not consider these jobs beneath him.

On one occasion the Guardian of the Franciscans who came to visit him, surprised him at this work [making sun-dried bricks]. . . . On one occasion a friar of importance came, it is not known of what Order, and [John] was working in the garden. It seemed that the visitor had found him thus engaged on other occasions, and he said to him: "[You] must be the son of some farmer since you like the garden so much that we never see you elsewhere." "I am not so important as that," replied Fray John, "for I am the son of a poor weaver." (Crisógono, *Life*, p. 211)

Pause: Ask yourself: Are there tasks that I consider beneath my dignity?

John's Words

John wrote the following words at the bottom of his sketch of Mount Carmel, a drawing that illustrated the straightest path to God's love.

> To arrive at being all
> desire to be nothing. . . .
> In this nakedness the spirit
> finds its rest, for when it
> covets nothing, nothing
> raises it up, and nothing
> weighs it down, because it is
> in the center of its humility.
> (John of the Cross, "The Ascent of Mount Carmel")

Reflection

During his days as a student, John studied in dark, poorly furnished rooms. Later, as prior, he chose small, cramped rooms, the poorest rooms in the monastery, as his quarters. The simple rooms that he preferred expressed his freedom of the soul. What was important for John was doing God's will and burning with love, not achieving social status or positions of honor.

The alternative to making our life into an expression of our own ambitions and will is to align ourselves with the will of someone greater—God. In doing so, we, like John, create an empty, inner room where God can enter, and we can rest in a truthful awareness of our dependency on God.

✧ Read the "About John" section in this meditation again. John was honest about how he saw himself. If you wanted someone to know who you were in all honesty and humility, what would you tell them? Try to tell this other person who you really are.

✧ Read the "John's Words" section again, praying slowly.

✧ Sometimes we pressure ourselves with goals, ambitions, and projects. We concentrate on "making things happen" or "doing things my way." List some of your goals, ambitions, and projects. Next, reflect on these questions: How do I really feel about the items on my list? Do I want these things because they are good for me or good for others? What role does God's will play in my ambitions?

✧ Write for fifteen minutes on your need to be in control of your life. Don't stop to think or revise, just write whatever comes to mind.

At the end of fifteen minutes, stop, meditate, and pray about what you wrote.

✧ Imagine that you are walking a country path. You come to a gate flanked by deep ravines. Examining the gate, you discover that it is locked and impossible to climb over. You realize that the gate is your own ego preventing you from peace with God and peace with yourself. How do you pass through the gate?

✧ Invite yourself to take a child's position before God. Imagine that you are a five-year-old sitting on Jesus' lap. Open your heart as a child would, and speak from the child within.

God's Word

An argument started between them about which of them was the greatest. Jesus knew what thoughts were going through their minds, and he took a little child whom he set by his side and then he said to them, "Anyone who welcomes this little child in my name welcomes me; and anyone who welcomes me, welcomes the one who sent me. For the least among you all is the one who is the greatest." (Luke 9:46–48)

Closing prayer: Read the following stanza from "The Ascent of Mount Carmel" as an expression of the deepest humility.

> I abandoned and forgot myself
> Laying my face on my beloved;
> All things ceased; I went out from myself,
> Leaving my cares
> Forgotten among the lilies.
> > (John of the Cross, "The Ascent of Mount Carmel")

The Ladder of Love

Theme: John used the image of a ladder to describe the journey of our soul to the infinite love of God. Each rung of the ladder teaches us new ways of love.

Opening prayer: My God, teach me to depend more and more on your love as I climb toward you.

About John

During his entire life, John climbed the ladder of love to God. At the close of his life, he reiterated that love was the only reason for life and the whole motivation for climbing the ladder to God.

"At the evening of life, you will be examined in love. Learn to love as God desires to be loved and abandon your own ways of acting." (P. 140)

On Friday, December 13, 1591, Fray Juan knew instinctively that his death was close at hand. He asked to see the prior and begged forgiveness for all the difficulties he had caused him and the monks. The prior made excuses for not being able to offer him more because of the poverty of the house. The day was silent and cold. Occasionally, Fray Juan would ask what time it was. He seemed obsessed with the time. He would then close his eyes. At times the brothers thought he had died, but no, he was only being quiet. When he opened his eyes he would look at the crucifix at his bedside, kiss it and go back into silence. . . .

. . . A few minutes later when the prior began saying the prayers for the dying person, Fray Juan asked him to read instead some passages from the *Song of Songs*. As they were read, he kept repeating: "What marvelous pearls! . . ." (Hardy, *Search for Nothing*, pp. 110–111)

So even at the very end, John heard the song of love. In death, he gave himself over into the hands of his Beloved.

Pause: Reflect on your life as a process of learning to love and your death as coming face to face with God's infinite love.

John's Words

For it is love alone that unites and joins the soul with God. To the end that this may be seen more clearly, we shall here indicate the steps of this Divine ladder one by one, pointing out briefly the marks and effects of each. . . .

. . . The first step of love causes the soul to languish [in love], and this to its advantage. . . .

The second step causes the soul to seek God without ceasing. . . .

The third step of the ladder of love is that which causes the soul to work. . . . Here, for the great love which the soul bears to God, it suffers great pains and afflictions because of the little that it does for God. . . .

The fourth step . . . is that whereby there is caused in the soul an habitual suffering because of the Beloved, yet without weariness. . . . In no way does the soul here seek its own consolation or pleasure. . . .

The fifth step of this ladder of love makes the soul to desire and long for God impatiently. . . .

On the sixth step the soul runs swiftly to God and touches Him again and again; and it runs without fainting by reason of its hope. For here the love that has made it strong makes it to fly swiftly. . . .

The seventh step of this ladder makes the soul to become vehement in its boldness. . . .

The eighth step of love causes the soul to seize Him and hold Him fast without letting Him go. . . . On this step of union the soul satisfies her desire, but not continuously. . . .

The ninth step . . . is that of the perfect, who now burn sweetly in God. . . .

The tenth and last step of this secret ladder of love causes the soul to become wholly assimilated to God, by reason of the clear and immediate vision of God which it then possesses. . . .

. . . By this mystical theology and secret love, the soul continues to rise above all things and above itself, and to mount upward to God. For love is like fire, which ever rises upward with the desire to be absorbed in the centre of its sphere. (John of the Cross, "The Dark Night")

Reflection

John's own experience of longing for love taught him about the ladder of love. For sincere seekers, the ascent goes something like this. The hunger for love draws the seeker to search for it. The heart grows restless, and one realizes that the created world will never completely satisfy the yearning. Then the seeker sacrifices willingly in answer to the call of love and lets go of attachments to things. The seeker becomes even more restless, and forgets his or her own self and concentrates on the burning desire for God. On the final steps of the ladder, nothing deters the longings of love, and the person swiftly and boldly moves toward union.

John invites us to embrace the process as grace calls us to it. God extends the promise of union with infinite love to those who persevere in the ascent. The process will cost us our attachments, compulsions, addictions, and even our life. But the culmination of the ascent is union with the God who is love.

✧ Slowly read the section "John's Words" again. If a phrase strikes you as particularly important, repeat it over and over, praying that the meaning will become clearer.

✧ Imagine you have only a few months to live. Would you be satisfied with your progress in loving God and the people in your life? Reflect on ways that you can increase your participation in the call to love. Express your love now, rather than waiting.

✧ Climbing the ladder of love results in a spiritual transformation. How has your life changed thus far in response to the love that has entered your life?
✦ Have you become less self-centered?
✦ Have you become more aware of your life and the lives of others as revelations of God's love for you?
✦ Have you discovered a greater willingness to love others unconditionally rather than a desire to possess them?

✧ The fire of love causes a hunger that cannot be satisfied until we are united with God. Meditate on these questions:
✦ Have you ever felt a restless yearning for love? When? How did you respond?
✦ When have you felt that nothing in this world would satisfy you completely except God's love?
✦ How could this intuition, if you accepted it as God's revelation to you, change your perspective on life?

✧ Write a letter to God describing your attempts to deepen your love.

✧ John tells us that our greatest need is to hold our tongues and speak to God in the silent language of love. Take time to be silent in God's presence. Let your heart's yearning find its way to God.

God's Word

Set me like a seal on your heart,
like a seal on your arm.
For love is strong as Death,
passion as relentless as Sheol.
The flash of it is a flash of fire,
a flame of Yahweh. . . .
Love no flood can quench,
no torrents drown.

(The Song of Songs 8:6)

Closing prayer:

My dear friends, we are already God's children,
but what we shall be in the future has not yet been
    revealed.
We are well aware that when [Jesus] appears
we shall be like him,
because we shall see him as he really is.

(1 John 3:2)

God is all love.

✧ For Further Reading ✧

Burrows, Ruth. *Ascent to Love: The Spiritual Teaching of St. John of the Cross*. Denville, NJ: Dimension Books, 1987.

The Collected Works of St. John of the Cross. Translated by Kieran Kavanaugh and Otilio Rodriguez. Washington, DC: ICS Publications, 1979.

Collings, Ross. *John of the Cross*. Vol. 10, *The Way of Christian Mystics*. Collegeville, MN: Liturgical Press, 1990.

Crisógono de Jesús. *The Life of St. John of the Cross*. Translated by Kathleen Pond. London: Longmans, Green & Co., 1958.

God Speaks in the Night: The Life, Times, and Teaching of St. John of the Cross. Translated by Kieran Kavanaugh. Washington, DC: ICS Publications, 1991.

Muto, Susan. *The Ascent: John of the Cross for Today*. Notre Dame, IN: Ave Maria Press, 1991.

Welch, John. *When Gods Die: An Introduction to John of the Cross*. Mawah, NJ: Paulist Press, 1990.

Acknowledgments (*continued*)

The poetry by John of the Cross on pages 13 (first excerpt), 13 (second excerpt), 19–20, 23 (first excerpt), 23 (second excerpt), 25, 26, 27, 28 (second excerpt), 28–29, 31, 41, 43–44, 46, 50 (third excerpt), 63–64, 66, 68, 69, 73, 75, 76, 79, 81, 89, 92, 94–95, and the excerpt on page 17 are from *John of the Cross: Selected Writings*, edited by Kieran Kavanaugh (New York: Paulist Press, 1987), pages 221, 298, 221, 220, 219, 298, 219, 293–294, 298, 295–296, 294, 222, 223, 226–227, 226, 219–220, 294, 57 and 59, 56–57, 55, 78–79, 78, 90–91, 96, 45, 56, and 14, respectively. Copyright © 1987 by Kieran Kavanaugh. Used by permission of Paulist Press.

The excerpts on pages 14, 15, 17, 19, 22, 24, 28, 32–33, 33, 37, 40–41, 42, 45, 49–50, 50 (first excerpt), 53, 54, 58 (first and second excerpt), 58 (third excerpt), 63 (first excerpt), 63 (second excerpt), 74, 80–81, 85 (first excerpt), and 88–89, are from *The Life of St. John of the Cross*, by Crisógono de Jesús, translated by Kathleen Pond (New York: Harper & Brothers, 1958), pages 3, 13, 71, 103, 303–304, 211, 265, 207, 207–208, 75–76, 254–255, 196, 149, 282, 288, 211, 132, 134, 75, 108, 138, 135, 267, 111, and 211, respectively. Permission applied for.

The excerpts on pages 18 and 20 are from *Spirit of Flame: A Study of St. John of the Cross*, by E. Allison Peers (New York: Morehouse-Gorham Co., 1944), pages 14 and 41, respectively. Copyright © 1944 by Morehouse-Gorham. Used with permission from SCM Press.

The excerpts on pages 36–37, 54, 67, 68, 93, 93–94, and the poetry by John of the Cross on page 50 second excerpt) are from *Search for Nothing: The Life of John of the Cross*, by Richard P. Hardy (New York: Crossroad, 1982), pages 14, 140, 66, 70, 140, 110–111, and 135, respectively. Copyright © 1982 by Richard P. Hardy. Reprinted by permission of the Crossroad Publishing Company.

The excerpts on pages 37 and 84 are from *St. John of the Cross*, by Bruno, edited by Benedict Zimmerman (New York: Sheed & Ward, n.d.), pages 290 and 4, respectively. Used with permission.

The excerpts on pages 70 and 76 are from *The Inner Eye of Love: Mysticism and Religion*, by William Johnston (New York:

The poetry by John of the Cross on page 85 is from *The Poems of St. John of the Cross*, translated by Roy Campbell (New York: Grosset & Dunlap, 1967), page 75.

The poetry by John of the Cross on pages 94–95 is from *Dark Night of the Soul*, translated by E. Allison Peers (Garden City, NY: Doubleday, 1959), pages 166–175.

Titles in the Companions for the Journey Series

Praying with Julian of Norwich

Praying with Francis of Assisi

Praying with Catherine of Siena

Praying with John Baptist de La Salle

Praying with Teresa of Ávila

Praying with Hildegard of Bingen

Praying with Ignatius of Loyola

Praying with Thérèse of Lisieux

Praying with Elizabeth Seton

Praying with Dominic

Praying with John of the Cross

Praying with Vincent de Paul   Available spring 1994

Praying with Thomas Merton   Available fall 1994

Order from your local religious bookstore or from

Saint Mary's Press
702 TERRACE HEIGHTS
WINONA MN 55987-1320
USA